'Unexpectedly captivating title undersells the valu thoughtful exploration o between work and the o capture the arc of careers and offer invaluable observations and advice in navigating the central relationships of our lives: family, work, and everything else.'

Stanley A. McChrystal, General, US Army (retired), Chairman & CEO, McChrystal Group

'A timely reminder that it's too easy to blame others rather than take ownership for your own career. And presented in such a refreshing, fun, and engaging format. A humorous murder mystery! Then again this is Drs S&O... I should expect nothing less!'

Trisha Conley, Executive Vice President People and Culture for LyondellBasell

'A much-needed guide for building resilience in the face of AI's rise. What stood out most to me was the book's belief in our ability to adapt – not just professionally, but as people.'

Ben Towers, CEO and Co-Founder Happl, Forbes 30 under 30

'I couldn't stop laughing and absolutely loved this book! It hilariously demystifies AI's role in our lives, bringing topics such as purpose and professional drift to life with a perfect blend of humour and insight. I must admit I was in stitches with the "ear caressing" part, but then again, who knows... I might have lost my marbles!'

Angelos Gkanoutas-Leventis, PhD, Dad, NED Greek Energy Forum, Low Carbon Advocate

'The *Devil Wears Prada* for AI geeks and novices.'

Dr Alison Edgar MBE, Author,
Entrepreneur, Start-Up Mentor

'A gripping and insightful exploration of professional survival in the AI era. *Artificial Death of a Career* blends storytelling with actionable wisdom. Schuster & Oxley craft a deeply relevant narrative that not only warns of obsolescence but also empowers readers with practical strategies to stay ahead. An essential read for anyone navigating the evolving job market.'

Felix Auböck, PhD Candidate, Olympic Finalist,
World and European Champion

'Book three in the Shey Sinope Saga is even more engaging and practical than *A Groundhog Career*. The first LGTBQ+ themed business book series. Courageous, illuminating, and simply brilliant!'

Daniel Fernando, Brazilian Engineer, educated in
London, Project Manager, Control and Technology
Enabler, Cyber Security Lead, Procurement Expert

'In the coming age of AI, and under the looming threat of loss of jobs, how do we think about our work life? Here is a book that reminds us that it is more important than ever to be agile, willing to reinvent yourself without losing your core purpose. This is a book not just about career advice but about life lessons.'

Vishaka N. Desai, Scholar, Teacher, Institution
Builder, former President of Asia Society, Senior
Advisor for Global Affairs Columbia University, Author
of the Award-Winning memoir 'World as a Family'

'This book gives a modern take on issues facing multiple generations of working people. As a student balancing work and studies, Shey's story really made me think about how easy it is to lose sight of what really matters, and that building a career shouldn't come at the cost of your support system.'

Zakaria Eltigani, Head of Finance Chirimoya, CEMS Master Programme

'One of the best pieces of advice I ever received was this: If, after two, five, or twenty years in your career, you're not learning something new, you're doing something wrong. This book captures that truth brilliantly, reminding us that every change is a challenge, and every challenge is an opportunity to grow.'

Ali Elsabagh, Co-Founder Scaleta, Youth Leader

'When Drs S&O warn about being the dodo among the chameleons, the lone bank teller among the ATMs, I felt like shouting, "and what about the last human illustrator drowning in a sea of prompted digital drivel?" But instead, I laughed and asked ChatGPT to write this soundbite.'

Andy 'Doodles' Baker, Illustrator, Animator, Father, Brummie, Game Show Contestant.

ARTIFICIAL DEATH OF A CAREER

OF A CAREER

A TALE OF PROFESSIONAL OBSOLESCENCE AND HOW TO AVOID IT

DR HELMUT SCHUSTER AND DR DAVID OXLEY

First published in Great Britain by Practical Inspiration Publishing, 2026

Book cover and illustrations by Andy 'Doodles' Baker.

The moral rights of the author have been asserted.

ISBN   9781788608060   (paperback)
        9781788608053   (hardback)
        9781788608077   (ebook)

EU GPSR representative: LOGOS EUROPE, 9 rue Nicolas Poussin, LA ROCHELLE 17000, France Contact@ logoseurope.eu

Want to bulk-buy copies of this book for your team and colleagues? We can customize the content and co-brand *Artificial Death of a Career* to suit your business's needs.

Please email info@practicalinspiration.com for more details.

Dedication

for Sue, without whom everything is less,
and
for Hermann, who taught me the power of thinking.

Contents

Introduction

This book addresses the threat of professional obsolescence. How can we navigate the waves of disruption that cause some professions to fall into decline and disappear. Indeed, how can we ensure that our professional skills, experience, and value remain relevant, useful, and in high demand over four decades or more?

In 2025, this subject is front of mind for many people. The spectre of artificial intelligence (AI) 'disrupting' more and more professions, vocations, and jobs has created headlines. In 2023, the Office for National Statistics reported a third of adults in the UK feared they might be in imminent threat of losing their jobs.[1] People in administrative, sales, and customer service jobs felt most vulnerable with 43% fearing redundancy within months. These concerns are fuelled by high-profile and well-reported projections from Goldman Sachs and McKinsey that AI has the potential to eliminate more than 300 million jobs by 2030.[2,3]

Of course, job insecurity is also influenced by 'normal' economic cycles. Major economies around the world are dealing with the consequences of, among other things, the effects of the COVID pandemic, globally significant armed conflicts, the rise of popularist isolationism (and trade wars), along with the lingering cost of the great financial crisis and the urgent need to find more sustainable sources of energy. All these factors, to use economist terms, influence the short- and long-term demand/supply curve of career opportunities.[4]

However, AI sets itself apart. Unlike the unwelcome but more familiar business cycles that cause occasional corporate rightsizing, AI has much more of an exotic, mysterious, malevolent air to it. Many of us have grown up with science fiction stories of errant robots and evil software. From HAL in *2001: Space Odyssey* to Skynet in *Terminator,* we have consumed a steady diet of scary stories that pit humans against technology. Perhaps, therefore, it should be no surprise that studies have found that over 90% of us currently believe AI to be an existential threat to our way of life.[5]

We don't set out in this book to directly investigate the facts and likely implications of AI on our lives over the next 10, 20, or 30 years. This said, it does provide us with a wonderful opportunity to discuss what separates those of us who are able to adapt, reimagine, and reinvent ourselves continually throughout our careers versus those who paint themselves more as helpless victims of an unfair professional world.

Is AI an existential threat? Perhaps. Does it present a greater threat than others we have successfully navigated over the past 200,000-plus years? In 2018, Sundar Pichai, Google's CEO, is reported to have said 'AI is one of the most important things humanity is working on. It's more profound than, I dunno, electricity or fire.'[6] We are sceptical of this claim. We would observe that humanity has a long history of navigating and ultimately benefiting from extraordinary discoveries and innovations. Consider, at the time of this book's publication, the following:

- 15 years ago, the iPhone was launched.
- 25 years ago, the first 'social' media site launched.
- 50 years ago, the internet was invented.

- 60 years ago, the personal computer was invented.
- 80 years ago, we harnessed the power of atomic power.
- 100 years ago, Turing machines and the age of computational devices began.
- 120 years ago, the Wright brothers flew 120 feet.
- 150 years ago, Alexander Graham Bell invented the telephone.
- 250 years ago, we navigated the industrial revolution.
- 270 years ago, Benjamin Franklin and his kite tripped across electricity.
- 600 years ago, Gutenberg invented the printing press.
- 1,100 years ago, gunpowder was invented in China.
- 1,300 years ago, the magnetic compass emerged as a means of navigation.
- 2,500 years ago, Pythagoras theorized the Earth was round.
- 5,500 years ago, writing emerged simultaneously in China, Mesoamerica, and the Middle East. Roughly at the same time, the wheel is said to have been first used in Lower Mesopotamia. (Interestingly, around the same time we discovered alcohol presumably because we then had Ox-Cart Uber transport to/from the pubs.)
- 150–200,000 years ago, language among humans evolved.
- 1.5 million years ago, we harnessed fire.

Each of these events ushered in a new era in our collective history. Like dominoes of progress, springboards into a new age, or (borrowing from Arthur C. Clarke) mysterious black monoliths.[7] Each had profound implications for how we lived, worked, interacted, and expanded the horizons of the possible. Our evolution and perhaps even survival as a species are intricately linked to our ability to discover new technology and adapt.[8] To paraphrase Darwin, 'it is not the most intellectual of the species that survives; it is not the strongest that survives but the species that survives is the one that is able best to adapt and adjust to the changing environment in which it finds itself.'[9]

We make the case that each disruptive wave not only thrusts our species forward but helps us hone our ability to navigate change over the long run. Ahead of each change, we feel a collective anxiety. A massive intake of breath. We seem to focus myopically on what may be 'lost' and are blind to new possibilities; like driving while only looking in the rear-view mirror. Despite this, we have an impressive track record, as a species, of reinventing ourselves. Looked at in this light, it's part of our genetic inheritance.

Our collective anxiety is a very natural and healthy thing. It is part of our built-in protective system. Our biological adaptation alarm clock, signalling loudly that it is time to wake up and take notice. What we sometimes refer to as the 'fight or flight' instinct, creating the required urgent insecurity that prompts action.[10] Researchers have referred to this as our 'survival optimization system'.[11]

So, if we have a track record, our societal trepidation is a healthy biological alarm, and continual adaptation is a necessary and good thing, then what's the big problem?

Well, if it were easy, everyone would do it!

This discussion about how humanity has adapted misses a key point. What about us… you and me? How do we ensure we aren't left behind? The Dodo among Chameleons. The Betamax among the VHS. The lone bank teller in a world of ATMs. The statistic that proves the point that change and adaptation is a *selective* process.

The consensus is that somewhere between 50% and 90% of us struggle to adapt to necessary change. PwC found that 63% of CEOs said their employees were unwilling or unable to adopt new systems. In the same survey, 44% of employees did not even acknowledge the importance of adaptation and continuous learning.[12] And of those of us that do recognize the need to learn something new, apparently only 50% of us make progress toward that goal.[13] Then, as reported by McKinsey, there is the depressing statistic that 70% of large scale organizational transformation programmes fail, with employee apathy a major factor.[14] And, to emphasize just how difficult we as individuals find changing behaviours even in the face of indisputable evidence of dire consequences, consider the startling fact that only 4% of people who suffered a near fatal heart attack were able to maintain the necessary changes in lifestyle (diet, exercise, etc.) required to prevent a repeat.[15]

So, how do we make ourselves resilient in the face of inevitable change? How do we make sure that we continually adapt and evolve? How do we stay relevant, necessary, and vital? How do we make sure that rather than fall by the wayside, we instead think of ourselves as skilled surfers able to ride each successive wave?

Someone should write a book about that…

Here is how we intend to take on the challenge. First, we discuss the risks of professional obsolescence. Of how, as we grow older, we must come to terms with juggling multiple priorities that may distract us from professional reinvention. Of giving in to the temptations of coming to believe we have 'earned' the right to 'dial-it-in'.

We will also look at how business life creates confusing choices about where to spend our time. At one level, this is navigating the tendency of larger organizations to get distracted by nice-to-do pet projects that aren't really value accretive. On another level, there are more nuanced questions about the intersection of our professional lives with the pull created by our growing awareness that there are other important things needing our attention.

Against these we contrast what we have learned from those people who frame their professional life as a continuous adventure. There are some distinct skills, behaviours, and habits that help them create a natural antidote to obsolescence – like a natural immunity against redundancy.

Ultimately, we make the case that continual reinvention is a choice. It is a behaviour, a set of habits, that constitute a distinct way of framing professional life. Consequently, it has the same challenges that might accompany any other major lifestyle change, like exercise, diet, creating a better work–life balance, strengthening personal relationships, or perhaps learning to speak a different language or play a musical instrument. Some of us find these things easier than others. But we can all do it. If we really want to. If we get the right encouragement, advice, coaching, and support.

Our goal in this book is to help you understand and build professional resiliency. To learn the tricks to making continual reinvention and adaptation an intrinsic part of who you are. To think of AI or the wave of change that naturally follows it, not as an unwelcome event that paralyzes you as you silently pray to be spared from its wrath, but as an opportunity to do something new, interesting, enlightening, and joyful. To approach adaptation not as a one-off event, but as something you continually strive for, search out even.

In summary, we advocate for and will help you build the capacity to be constructively restless, an avid professional adventurer, seeking and finding fulfilment by learning and exploring. Not so much to 'boldly go where no one has gone before' but to discover the joy and fulfilment in continually challenging yourself to push the boundaries of what you believe you are capable of.

This book has two parts. In Part I, we tell the story of Shey Sinope. For those of you who have read our previous books, you will recognize Shey. He is now in his late 30s and navigating a new phase in his professional life. Our story centres on the themes we have discussed in this Introduction, and yes, there is both an AI theme and a murder/mystery to enjoy. We may doubt some of the hype about evil AI software taking over the world, but it does make for a good story.

For those of you who haven't read our previous books, we would first suggest you correct that momentous omission. However, let us reassure you, this book is designed to provide you with a completely fulfilling experience as a stand-alone. If, as we sincerely hope, you enjoy the latest instalment in Shey's journey, you can go back and read the previous stories later.

In Part II, we deconstruct the main themes of allowing your career and professional relevance to fall into obsolescence and how we can build the skills and behaviours that will make us more resilient and better able to constantly reinvent our professional lives. We share case studies from some extraordinary people whose stories amplify the points we make. Each chapter ends with some thinking and coaching exercises and closes with our version of a *blink* summary.

Finally, before we close our Introduction, we think we should answer an important question. Perhaps you are browsing this Introduction in the bookstore debating whether to invest your time and money in this book. We think that's a very reasonable question. If you have read this far, we will presume you have already decided that our subject matter is of interest to you. All that remains is to address the questions of whether we, Drs Schuster & Oxley, are the right thought partners for you. So, let us try to answer that.

First, you might look at our educations, our doctoral training, related research, and that might make you comfortable that we have a very good grounding in the behavioural science that underpins the challenges of navigating a fulfilling career.

Equally, you might look at the 80-plus articles we have authored on careers and the world of work over the past two years. We have dedicated ourselves to researching and writing highly accessible articles on what we believe are the big career issues of the current era. Our particular focus is on helping individuals understand and optimize their professional experience. We have had plenty to discuss with the backdrop of the COVID pandemic, digital revolution, changing corporate and entrepreneurial road maps, as well as regulatory and political shifts. To the extent you find it reassuring, our advice has made it on to the BBC Business News and into *The Times*, *Forbes*, *Fast Company*, *People Management*, *Big Think*, *Readers Digest*, and even *The Sun* and *Daily Star*.[16]

Alternatively, you might prefer to look at our commercial credentials and experience. A greater emphasis on doing? We have both navigated 40-year executive and board-level careers in consulting, fast-moving consumer goods, commodity trading, and energy. We have worked with some extraordinary leaders in the UK, USA, India, Middle East, and continental Europe. In the process, we like to think we helped those leaders and the businesses they led achieve some impressive results. Much of our work involved optimizing individual and team performance, and, like many professional sports coaches might also observe, the secret to extraordinary performance started with helping individuals become the best version of themselves.

Perhaps these explanations provide you with sufficient reassurance. However, we have entered this writing collaboration with a purpose and goal that is a bit different than simply pointing to our past training, prior publications, and professional experience. After all, your goals, challenges, and circumstances will be unique. There will be some common themes and challenges but how *you* choose to navigate them should be completely personal to *you*. So, our aim with this book is to be more of a mentor or coach. Your personal thought partner or sounding board. The big distinction with this book is to think about things that are difficult to talk about elsewhere. Things that we, over the years, have been conditioned to believe we must either ignore or deny. The doubts and insecurities we can't be open about with society, community, family, friends, and work colleagues for fear of harsh judgement.

So, our aim is to create a safe space for us to discuss questions that may be difficult for you to find another outlet to work through. And, therefore, while it may sound strange, we think the main criteria for investing your time in this book is that we might be surprisingly good listeners.

Now, enough of the build-up, *Artificial Death of a Career* follows. We hope you enjoy the story as much as we have enjoyed writing it.

Part I
Artificial Death
of a Career

Chapter 1

Hey El... Write Me a Bio

'Hey, El, can you write me a biography for this conference? They want a couple of paragraphs?'
'Sure, Shey, how about this?'

Shey Sinope, 37, is a US educated tech entrepreneur now based in London. He is most famously associated with the FEEL VR emotional amplifier headband launched to great fanfare five years ago. The media buzz following FEEL VR's launch propelled Shey to the forefront of the vibrant UK tech start-up scene with his name increasingly a genericide for everything AI... an Anglo-mini-me version of USA's Sam Altman. Unlike Sam, however, Shey has typically shied away from the public spotlight, a factor that has only cemented his position in technology folklore.

Shey built his early career at MGL Mania, a deep learning consulting, design, and project management company. It was during his time at MGL Mania that he joined forces with Emi Silva and Ellen Elpis to develop the very first protypes of FEEL VR. The first version wowed the tech community not so much for its aesthetics as its ingenious recycling of legacy components. The prototype was said to cost just $200 to build. An extraordinary achievement for someone juggling a full-time job and in what seemed like a mind-boggling short proof of concept period.

Shey now spends his time focusing on the high-level strategic stewardship of FEEL VR which operates one of the first almost completely auto-mated manufacturing, production, retail, and customer service platforms, driven by the power-ful but very secret Shey Sinope designed AI.

An intensely private and guarded person, little is known of Shey's private life, beyond his work to protect and further LGBTQIA+ causes and his generous support for refugee human rights.

He is also, not a giraffe.

'Very funny. Thanks. It's a good start. I'll make a few tweaks and send it off,' Shey responded cheerfully.

Chapter 2

Artificial Outrage

'… and this is why we don't need just a pause in the use and reckless development of AI – we need to regulate it, contain it, ban it. The greatest problem with AI is that we aren't scared enough of it! Atomic energy, hydrogen bombs we know have the power to kill millions, destroy civilization for generations.' Dr 'Tiny' Banty was building to his grand finale. Over the past few years, he had honed his AI stage debate patter. The public talking circuit had proven lucrative. In fact, between his two best-selling books, podcast, and paid talking engagements, Tiny was raking it in.

'Many of you unquestionably accept climate change results from human actions. You have no difficulty swallowing the argument that we are imminently in danger of reaching a tipping point beyond which large parts of our world will be uninhabitable. Even the simple pleasures of individual choice and freedom that accompany smoking tobacco or owning an AR15 – I know many of you climb on your mountains of indignance, looking down, and shaking your heads with righteous cries for bans and regulation. My point is simple, *ladies* and *gentlemen*.' He made a point of emphasizing the gender pronouns. This was his favourite part. He heard a drum roll in his head. 'Unlike some of the more questionable encroachments that our government makes to limit our liberties and curtail our freedoms, making AI illegal would actually *for once* be justifiable.

'Let me recount again why… first, at an all too real individual level, AI robs the most vulnerable among us of making a living wage. Unlike the silly gender politics of our times, AI discriminates by making a few entrepreneurs, like my opponent today, obscenely rich while making the rest of us increasingly marginalized and diminished. The platitudes about AI empowering are rubbish, a smoke screen, concocted by those who use AI to subjugate us as they become the industrial robber barons of this century. Let me remind you of the consequences. All of the power in our economic system will be increasingly controlled by an uber rich super elite, who will use their resources to pervert our political systems to ensure they consolidate and protect their interests.

'If this isn't scary enough, *they know not what they do!* As they develop these AI systems, as they brazenly, unconscionably, and unforgivably, openly acknowledge… they don't know how their models work! They are black boxes. Extraordinarily sophisticated BUT not understood AIs that are being given control… CONTROL… *ladies* and *gentlemen*… of EVERY aspect of our lives. Health care, transportation, banks, government… MILITARY! The goal is simple – making money. Efficiency. Productivity. Not humanity, society, or greater good. Profit is all that matters. How can we trust that these new digital robber baron industrialists will not fall foul of the hubris and avarice that has infected all *great men* throughout time. Power corrupts and absolute power corrupts absolutely.

'And finally, the big one. Skynet. HAL9000. The Matrix. The greatest technical minds of our time – Musk, Gates,

Wozniak, Yang – people who know what they are talking about. They all point out that when, not if, AI becomes "self-aware", we must assume the worst. As Kurzweil famously predicts, the age of super-intelligent machines is not 50 years away, its less than ten. And once we cross that line… there is no turning back. No putting the genie back in the bottle. And what if this inevitable super intelligence concludes humanity is a pest, a bug, a parasite on the world, or even just an inconvenience? I'll tell you…' He paused and dramatically snapped his fingers right in front of the microphone. The reverb around the packed auditorium was deafening. 'We… cease… to… exist.

'An AI with access to the world's resources.' He looked at the camera and gave a dramatic despairing shrug. 'Sure, it could be a nuclear Armageddon but it's likely to be far more subtle than that. After all, why blow up the world when you just want to eliminate one annoying species. No, it will more likely be water or food supply, a virus, a bioweapon, or my favourite… just reprogramming our cars to drive off cliffs.[1]

'*Ladies* and *gentlemen*… in the history of time, since Adam and Eve were tempted by the snake, there has never been a more urgent and immediate existential threat to humanity… to all of us… than AI. Please join me in supporting the motion… The United Nations should immediately place the same restrictions on AI as it does to chemical weapons, land mines, and liquids of over 100ml in carry-on luggage!'

As Tiny turned to take his seat on the dais, the conference room echoed with applause and cheers. A thunderous round of chants rang out… 'Make America Analogue Again. Put the might back into Ludd again! King Cnut is Cute! Let's make our age a new STONErs age!'

Shey Sinope scanned the room. He knew this was a mistake. He typically declined these requests to appear on the conference circuit. There were lots of reasons why they didn't appeal. He was a natural introvert. He'd always preferred the company of a computer or server over large groups of people. He found he processed information better when he could sit and think about a subject. Generally, he didn't find it easy to spontaneously react to a question or provocation. He had always envied the people who could think so quickly on their feet. Apparently able to conjure complex arguments and justifications from some secret compartment in their brain. Often, he wasn't sure what his opinion or view might be until he'd been able to reflect on it for several minutes. He clearly wasn't a natural fit for something like this. So, why was he here? It was all El Gin's fault. They had pushed him to do it. Over the past few years, the requests to appear at public events had come in and he had rejected them all. However, as his FEEL VR business had become increasingly popular, at least in the unicorn tech start-up space, the requests kept coming.[2] In fact, his reluctance to appear had increased the clamour from conference organizers. It was almost like there was now something of a competition to be the first to land him as a keynote speaker.

El had also been working on Shey. Slowly eroding his resistance. 'It will be fine,' they said. 'Think of all the free publicity. All the earned media. All the vloggers live streaming and the geek fan-people. They love to nerd out on what you say, what you really mean, and obsess over the tiniest "easter egg" clues they believe might be encoded in your words. Just think what fun we could have!' It was a persuasive argument. If only he didn't have to stand on a stage and give a presentation. He hated presentations. It was as if his body threw a hidden switch about five minutes before he was due to present. One that resulted in his body no longer responding to commands from his brain. His core body temperature went thermo-nuclear, and his hands started to shake. And something strange happened to his voice. He sounded like a warbling bird.

But it was more than this. He was fed up with being alone, isolated. The COVID pandemic might now be five years in the past, but its legacy was profound. The work from home (WFH), hybrid work arrangements had proven annoyingly resilient. In fact, in their own way, Shey thought, they were a more powerful virus. One fuelled by self-serving justifications and a sense of entitlement. The lifestyle tail wagging the business and employment dog. Shey was an introvert, yes. But he still needed to be around people just not always talking or interacting with them. Social but in a specifically introverted form. He had come to think being anti-social was only effective when you have people close by to ignore. One reason he accepted the conference invitation was to escape his living room, to commune with other humans in person and not via a monitor.

The *Las Vegas Artificial Intelligence Annual Symposium* was the biggest in the calendar. Biggest in terms of audience. Some 5,000 journalists, tech leaders, venture capitalists, investors, and probably a handful of disorientated partygoers. The keynote speakers got paid, all expenses were covered, and there was a guarantee of huge media hype. The main event of the conference was a faux debate. Apparently, even more theatrical and contrived than Shey had expected. The organizers posed a question, and two hyped-up speakers would attempt to sway a vote for or against. Sort of like an AI equivalent of Stephen Fry against the Catholic Church but with less talented or charismatic public speakers.[3] Two big digital screens either side of the stage live streamed the debate with an overlay of social media commentary and second-by-second updates on how the audience sentiment was leaning.

However it had happened, Shey found himself seated in front of this raucous crowd. He looked over at the screen nearest him. Apparently Tiny had 70% of the audience with him. Shey shook his head. This was depressing; it made him angry. This was supposed to be a gathering of industry insiders. AI experts. How could they buy the utter BS that this Tiny guy just sold them. Shey realized that his indignation was helping him overcome his stage fright. He leaned into the emotion.

The moderator of the conference quelled the noise and began their introduction of Shey. There were the familiar cliches about unicorns, user adoption, technology innovation, and of course use of AI as an engine of growth. Shey focused on the podium ahead of him. He imagined Tiny's pompous face in front of it. Everything else faded. Shey put his speaking notes down on the table beside him and strode toward the rostrum. He gently pushed the moderator to one side.

'I'd like to interest you all in some land I have available for sale. Yes, I think you'll all be interested. Fantastic unobstructed views. The weather is amazing with very warm days and cool nights. Zero humidity. No planning permission restrictions. Build whatever you like. If you like solitude, its perfect for you, 240,000 miles away from your nearest neighbour. Lacks a little atmosphere perhaps, but you guys can put that right. But here is the big one, I guarantee you will be off grid! Free from the clutches of AI. Show of hands… any takers?' Shey scanned the room. There were one of two hands but generally people looked more confused.

'OK. How about this… how many of you know that the word "gullible" doesn't actually appear in the dictionary? Again, raise of hands?' One or two who had recently discovered long lost Nigerian relatives raised their hands.

'I do find it fascinating that we seem all too ready to debate whether the Moon landings were real, whether the Earth is in fact flat, or as my slippery, manipulative, morally, and ethically bankrupt, self-satisfied opponent alluded to, that climate change isn't a direct consequence of humanity's choice to satisfy meaningless consumption regardless of the cost. It is extraordinary to me that we seem so ready to enthusiastically and endlessly dissect these matters of scientific consensus, and yet apparently so willing to accept Dr Banty's wafer-thin appeals to our base emotions.' Shey surveyed the now subdued room. 'We are better than this. I know we are.

'Dr Banty offered four empty and meaningless urban myths to persuade you that we should run from continuing to develop AI. In simple terms, they were all based on the same warped logic – rationalizations that the world's frightened incumbents have used to justify repressing EVERY major human innovation throughout history. In short, it feels like a threat to how we live our lives today… therefore, it is evil… in the immortal words of Monty Python… it's a Witch![4]

'When you think about human history, every one of the major phases of our development as a civilization has been met with fear, resistance, repression, even persecution. Unscrupulous people fuel our collective anxieties by offering half-baked conspiracy theories that turn our natural instinctive anxieties into full-blown fear. Dr Banty and all those who argue against AI aren't new or even novel. They join a long list of people throughout time. Like a Newtonian reaction to the powers of progress from Leonardo Di Vinci, through Darwin and Oppenheimer, they become the equal and opposite force. Our contemporary Luddites.

'The main challenge to responding to Dr Banty's arguments is that it is infantile. It is playground stuff. Like someone who stands in front of you and stubbornly demands you disprove that day is night or that black is white. They drag you down and mischievously force you to debate the absurd.

'Tech businesses and entrepreneurs *aren't* interested in subjugating, controlling, or repressing anyone. They *are* interested in developing products and services that society needs. That solve a problem. This is how capitalism works. If they do that well, their companies will succeed. If they do that poorly, they will fail. While we should always be willing to debate consequences, particularly unintended ones, authentic debates seem to get hijacked by politicians, celebrities, and professional debate performers attempting to sell us tin foil hats. This is a "look at the invisible sparkling jewel in my left hand and pay no attention as my right hand removes your wallet" tactic.

'Part of his first argument was the implicit threat of personal disruption that comes along with any major leap forward in technology. However, Dr Banty presented this as some sort of choice. As if big tech was deciding to cause some of you the pain of redundancy and job elimination. The bad news is that AI will likely result in some jobs going away. What he conveniently omits however is that it will also create millions of jobs. How you frame the disruption to existing jobs caused by AI is important. Objectively, we have weathered similar disruptions every 50 years or so. We have proven our resilience, and I have no doubt we will prove so again.

'The third argument was an extraordinary twist on reality. Advances in machine learning, on the sophisticated software algorithms built on neural nets, that have been pioneered by ChatGPT, Gemini, Perplexity, DeepSeek, etc., help dramatically improve the quality, consistency, speed, and efficiency of decision making. The reason AI is so appealing is that it simply does things better than existing systems. Ask yourself the question, do you want your medical scans interpreted with 85% or 99% accuracy? Do you want to wait 12 months for the surgery you need, or 12 days? What about your elderly relatives, would you welcome a solution that helps them grow older with dignity, with better quality of life, in their own homes? And education… how about one-to-one teaching ratios?

'However, these examples miss the real point of advances in this field. It's the new possibilities that are more exciting than improving on how we do things today. Solving climate change. Curing cancer. Solving food and water supply. Helping humans live consistently beyond 100 years. Taking scarcity and creating abundance. Even exploring and colonizing our solar system. Why wouldn't we want this? Why would we say thanks but no thanks… I'd prefer to stay right here!?

'Perhaps the reason, as Dr Banty so cynically attempted to exploit, is our human scepticism. He played on our fears that we may lose something precious and irreplaceable. The crux of this doubt, this anxiety, is our selfish gene. The worry that while something might be good for humanity, society, our community, it might be a threat to us personally. Like the thinking that promotes protectionism across the world. We are quick to support systematic improvements, until they knock on our front door and ask us to adjust our routines. And yet, ultimately, what do they say about progress? It is both relentless and inevitable. Those union workers who strike to prevent automation adoption at best delay the inevitable but at worst promote the opportunity for a start-up to bypass them completely.

'And so… we are left only with Dr Banty's existential scare mongering. Is AI an extinction threat to humanity? My simple answer is *no*. When we talk about the technology today, we are really referring to very narrow forms of AI. Software models that are essentially very sophisticated decision and logic trees. I find it very hard to see how the existing models could ever become, whether intentionally or by accident, the self-aware Skynet Hollywood incarnations that are so often cited as a justification for resisting progress. Those of us who use machine learning generative AI models are excited about its *possibilities* but are also very aware of its *limitations*.

'All of these models are just more and more sophisticated widget makers. They address a human input. A question. They serve to solve a specific problem. Like Douglas Adams' *Deep Thought*, the question defines, restricts, and limits what follows.[5] These existing models don't work without first being given a very narrow problem to solve. Asking them to solve the answer to life, the universe and everything will get you nowhere.

'And, ultimately, this is the big misconception, a matter of exaggeration and nefarious manipulation, not reality. It's a fear of the words being used rather than the facts. Like being scared of the dark or the word "moist". The latest iterations of AI have been reported as coming close to mirroring the 86 billion neurons in our human brains. This is wrong though, a misleading statistic. It is a mistake to think of the increasing number of neural network nodes as a proxy for human self-awareness and analogous to true general AI. The myth and misconception are fuelled by websites, newspapers, and bad actors, like Dr Banty. The way these existing models work is much more like a lot of labrador brains. Ask yourself, really, what would happen if we were able to wire the brains of 1,000 labradors together? Would we get some omnipotent super intelligence? No... of course not. It doesn't matter how many labradors you wire up...

all you will get are increasingly sophisticated attempts to acquire more dog biscuits.

'So… I guess if you're scared of cookies… vote with Dr Banty… Oh wait… Tiny Banty… how apt. Banty… chicken. That's hilarious. OK people, I have an overwhelming desire to find a big American oatmeal raisin cookie. I bet in Las Vegas they are as big as a house!' Shey looked around the room to a stunned silence. He took that as his cue and exited stage right.

೮೦೮౩

'Well, that went well.'

'You think so?' Shey was hoping for some reassurance. He was at the airport about to board his flight.

'Yes. Absolutely. The social media reaction is off the chart. I monitored X, Instagram, TikTok, Facebook. The references to Shey Sinope, AI debate, Las Vegas AI Symposium, are astronomical. You are trending, viral, everyone is talking about you,' replied El cheerfully.

'OK. But is that a good thing? Is that what we wanted?'

'Yes! Our metrics on the PR scorecard are at all-time highs. I have identified some similar events for you to consider. There are also multiple media enquiries competing for interviews. The goal was to get FEEL VR maximum impact, as quickly and cost effectively as we could. I'd say mission accomplished.'

'El, as a matter of interest, what other words are trending alongside our coverage?'

'Unhinged, Rant, and Chicken Little, appear the most. There's also a lot of searches for "is the word gullible in the dictionary?" and "how smart are super smart labradors?"' El replied, again very cheerfully.

Chapter 3

Stoicheion Deduction

Angelos Herodotus grew up on the Island of Hydra off the Athenian coast. The island had been a haven for pirates in the fifteenth and sixteenth centuries. It had prospered as the skilled mariners picked off the wealthy vessels shuttling between Venice, Italy, Greece, and the eastern Mediterranean. The island was cleverly camouflaged to avoid detection by passers-by. As Angelos grew up, he was immersed in the rich history and heritage of this maverick privateer independence and the intoxicating romance of ancient Greek history. As a boy he would help shepherd the donkeys as they did their job delivering goods from the small port. The island was home to thousands of small businesses mainly catering to a growing tourist trade. Unlike the other Greek islands, however, Hydra appealed to a more reclusive, wealthier visitor. Counting Leonard Cohen and David Gilmore among its part-time residents.

While Angelos was indelibly marked by his idyllic childhood, his future career path was profoundly shaped by three other things. First, his father was a world renown commercial lawyer. Second, he was prodigiously bright with an extraordinary memory for detail. Angelos could remember the weather and what he had for breakfast on any given day of his life. A trick he would often perform for his friends. August 12, 2003… Sunny and 30°C… olives and feta cheese. February 19, 2008… Sunny and 25°C… Greek salad. Admittedly, the recall trick was a little less impressive when you understood the limited variation in both weather and diet.

However, by far the biggest influence on Angelos was his neighbour, a Mr Scaramanga. He spent hours in the company of the old man with his distinctive slicked back grey hair, unusual penchant for three-piece suits, and gaudy gold jewellery. Scaramanga told the most mesmerizing stories of solving famous crimes in exotic locations. As Angelos grew older and followed his prescribed path to one of London's top law schools and then London's famed Magic Circle legal fraternity, his distance from Hydra grew, as did his lament for the glory, glamour, and romanticism of the world seen through Scaramanga's eyes. Was it coincidence that his namesake appeared in some of the great spy novels of the 20th century? The evidence seemed to suggest so. But was there ever such a thing as pure coincidence? Perhaps it was wishful thinking, but the idea of hidden, unsolved mysteries lingered, inspired, and excited his imagination.

And so it was that Angelos came to live dual lives. During the day he was Angelos Herodotus, the formidable, extraordinarily expensive, very exclusive lawyer. At night, Angelos spent most of his evening in the company of similarly accomplished but repressed detective wannabes at the secret 221B Baker Street Club located in a discreet room at one of London's oldest private clubs.

Chapter 4

It's Only Business

A week had passed since his Las Vegas performance. The memory had faded as the week's busy routine of hustle and bustle had unfolded. Shey looked around his living room come home office. He reflected on how professional life had begun to ape the wider world. A few years earlier he remembered making caustic observations about corporate warriors sleepwalking through life in their 'phubbles'. It was like they anesthetized themselves against the banal realities of corporate life by immersing themselves in imaginary personal force fields. He would watch them at his local coffee shop, head down, eyes glued on something strangely fascinating on their phone screens. The irony of social media creating social isolation. He conjured the term 'phubble' to sneer at their behaviour, the lengths they were prepared to go to ensure no one intruded on their personal space, the small adjustments they made to ensure there was at least six feet of space between them and everyone else, and above all, their incredibly annoying insistence of navigating around without ever looking up from their phone screens. Shey would deliberately keep walking toward these phubble prisoners on a collision path, playing a private game of chicken.

So, it's even more ironic, he thought. *It's almost like the world has conspired to drag me into a phubble... just one that involved my apartment living room, my laptop, my Amazon-acquired ergonomic desk, and my essential three-speed massaging chair with cooling and heating options.* The COVID pandemic had created a hasty mass migration to remote working. After the worst of the pandemic, for technology companies at least, the case for office work had proven hard to reassert.

For Shey, however, the business productivity arguments for work colleagues to spend time together in the office didn't adequately address the wider personal feeling of isolation and loneliness. He had recently been reflecting on how after years of studies we had come to accept the wisdom of Seasonal Affective Disorder (SAD), the phenomenon of how our body's circadian rhythm left us more susceptible to depression in winter.[1] He speculated that in 10 or 20 years, we would come to accept that the WFH craze would lead to the discovery of a *Virtual Isolation Disorder* in a similar vein. The trouble was that despite all the wishfulness and barely veiled delight with which many people greeted the unexpected opportunity to WFH, at least for Shey, it robbed him of the sense of support and *esprit de corps*. The unintended consequence of people now jealously and self-servingly finding reasons to defend what they saw as an unexpected work–life windfall might well lead to greater levels of depression and mental health crises.

We really aren't very good at balancing the short and long term, Shey thought. *It's like the temptation to cut in line or buy the black-market product at a huge discount. We choose not to think it all the way through. When it comes to WFH, things that we barely noticed, like the ability to empathize and vent to a colleague about something trivial, well, you only realize how important it is when something breaks down the road.*

Shey felt fortunate to have escaped the corporate hamster wheel. He was no longer a prisoner of a salary. He launched his own business, FEEL VR, some seven years earlier. After an anxious and stressful interlude of juggling entrepreneurial life with the safe but oppressive suffocation of corporate life, he had made the leap into entrepreneurship. Those first few years were intoxicating, exhausting, exhilarating, eye-opening, liberating but, at the same time, a whole new level of responsibility and commitment. It was all worth it. He had new degrees of freedom, fewer constraints, as well as an absence of rules and processes.

His FEEL VR business had done well. With the moral support of Emi Silva and Ellen Elpis, he had navigated three rounds of fundraising and was now dreaming about IPOs and strategic partnerships. The main product was a virtual reality headset that was designed to give users simulated emotions while they used social media apps. Shey had conceived the product as an antidote to the negative aspects of social media. User feedback had been excellent, but business execution was always tricky and thankless. Fortunately, he had some very sophisticated AI software that helped him manage most things.

Emi Silva had chosen to stay at MGL Mania, Shey's old employer, where they had first met. He was now a senior executive and by all accounts very happy with life. Ellen, well, Shey missed Ellen the most. She had been volunteering at a humanitarian NGO trying to make a difference with health care and food supplies in Palestine. Shey's admiration for Ellen had only grown over the years. Her energy, passion, determination, and resilience were extraordinary. Yet, she was never judgemental of other's choices and was always willing to listen, even when, by comparison, the problems must have seemed, well, rather trivial. She did Ellen. She didn't preach about it. She tried to fix what she thought needed fixing. She operated on a more global, altruistic scale than most others. Where once Shey had cynically dismissed Ellen as naïve and hopelessly romantic, he now saw her as a beacon of human compassion. She was an example of humanity on its very best day.

Shey had made the transition from corporate warrior to entrepreneur. He now fully embraced his new identity. And, fuelled by a deep sense of conviction that FEEL VR could make a dent in the world, a positive one, he had committed to the journey. In fact, his progress hadn't gone unnoticed. As the buzz about FEEL VR had grown, so had the invitations to contribute to and even join other start-ups. He currently, technically, was a director or advisor to five additional businesses, all in the AI space. All of them came with investors, management teams, and boards. In each case there was a strange ambiguity between board chairpersons, the lead investors, the major suppliers, and the businesses founder/CEOs all being his 'boss'. Most of the time it was a good thing. But sometimes, when something went wrong, it was a game of pin the tail on the donkey trying to figure out who was supposed to be accountable.

On balance, though, it was better than the alternative. He got comfortable with how the start-up culture of burning cash to build viability worked. Of strangers thrusting money at him and telling him to 'speculate to accumulate'. Sometimes it was a bit overwhelming and confusing. Occasionally, he needed to remind himself, though, to assert some authority, impose his will on something. It helped him feel better and masked his growing worry that he had begun to drift... he had a sense that the routine was a sedative. Work wasn't as much fun as it used to be. And life seemed, well, more complex.

So, for example, WFH… if he really didn't like it, he could do something about it. Shey had come to think that his position afforded certain privileges. He had access to resources, to money. Surely, he should use those resources when he could to do some good. All the better if he could champion a just cause and make him feel better about the humdrum of business at the same time. Shey took pride in some of those small victories. Of being on the right side of history. Of making himself available to those who had questions, problems, issues, concerns. He tried very hard to be the boss he never had. And as FEEL VR's founder, CEO, and significant shareholder, well, he could set the policies that he thought made sense.

'Hey, El, what's next on the calendar today?'

'You have a video conference with Jian Xu in five,' El replied.

'Did I know about that? What's the agenda?' Jian was FEEL VR's new chairperson and was appointed by the company's biggest new shareholder.

'I'm sorry, Shey I'm afraid I can't share any details,' El said mysteriously.

'That's strange. He's normally so formal about these things. No worries, it must be about the status report and update I sent him last week.'

Just then Shey's computer screen binged with the familiar sound of an incoming video call. Shey put on his headphones, adjusted the microphone, switched on his 4k camera, and powered up the three strategically placed LED refracted lights. One of the by-products of working from home so much over the last few years was the significant and continuous pursuit of high-quality video and audio. Honestly, there was no excuse nowadays not to have at least Instagram if not full-blown regional TV level production standards.

'Mr Sinope, *ho ware* you?' Jian must have just jumped off a call with his Chinese colleagues. His accent was always more exaggerated when he first switched.

'Fine… fine. I know we have not spoken for a few weeks. Not sure why. I did want to give you an update on my latest changes and progress at FEEL VR.' Shey jumped straight into his spiel. 'As you know, I plan to send out the return to the office mandate. I want all key personnel back in the office at least three days a week starting from next month. It's time to just rip that band-aid off.'

'Well… I'm…'

'Also,' Shey continued, 'I think in part to balance the messaging, I plan to announce the new employee benefits enhancements. I've had a few requests from different people for support on a raft of what seem like reasonable refinements to our offer. So, I'll go ahead and confirm FEEL VR will now reduce the standard work week to a four-day week. This will erode any resistance to the return to the office mandate.' Shey paused. Yes, that was a solid approach but whatever the cost, he was determined to end WFH.

'I also have a few other things I'm going to change. Just FYI. I plan to allow all employees unlimited paid time off subject to managerial approval, provide the annual health club sponsorship of $10,000 per year, adoption and IVF subsidies of $5,000 per child, along with a year's paid parental leave, of course.

'I'm also very concerned about how the world seems to have taken a dark turn on LGBTQIA+ matters. So, I plan to make FEEL VR a champion for inclusive causes both inside the company and on a local and national stage. I'd like to sponsor positive ad campaigns on social media to raise awareness and counter the rising hate, particularly misogyny and homophobia. It's really important for us to stand up for what we believe.

'I'm proud to say, we have just shipped out the latest medicine, food, and water package to Gaza. Of all the things we've done so far this year, this I am certain has had the most impact. My friend Ellen tells me that the reality on the ground is still absolute hell. However, we have helped save lives.' Shey couldn't help but feel a difficult to label warm glow when he thought of these humanitarian outreach efforts.

'Oh, I've been contacted by a local not-for-profit theatre group who need some funds to help them continue to put summer musical shows on in Regent's Park. I attended Matilda last year and it was amazing.

Completely free for anyone who wants to attend. It was idyllic. Picnics on the lawn. Some incredibly talented performers and production quality. My partner is auditioning for Widow Twankey in the Aladdin pantomime. Really $100,000 is nothing to us and we will get great community good will.'

'Shey, Mr Sinope, this is most surprising.' Shey did not pick up on Jian's tone.

'I know. I am convinced FEEL VR will be the envy of the tech start-up space.' Shey paused to picture himself sharing a joke and reminiscing with Ellen and Emi about old times. About how far they'd come. How life had changed so much for them all. He felt a little like an entrepreneurial Father Christmas, although he preferred to think of himself as a more benevolent Steve Jobs or more empathetic Elon Musk. Why can't I succeed in business while doing some good along the way, he sometimes mused, rehearsing for the day that Walter Issacson interviewed him.

'But… I and the board, and Shanghai XXVC, we have concerns… the targets and milestones are not met some time since 12 months.'

'Oh, I'm not worried about that. It's not that important. I'm sure you've seen our latest valuation report. As long as the VC market stays strong, we should continue to have multiple sources of new capital. Anyhow, growth is important but not everything.' Shey didn't expect to have to spell out the obvious. He had learned over the past five years that the tech start-up space was less about profit and cash flow and more about the forward story. If you could point to huge potential untapped users, and a plausible path to acquire them, the capital faucets seemed to flow.

'Well… it is difficult, but we must we think make a change. We have become aware of issues. Cash flow remains negative. Customer acquisition costs increasing. Most importantly, new active user growth has decreased in last report. We now believe real risk we won't hit exit strategy criteria. Investors and board believe bold we must be… before it's too late and we lose momentum. Momentum… very important. Must remain positive.' This was unusually direct. Jian clearly was feeling the heat from someone.

'Now wait. Is this about that silly Las Vegas thing? I was persuaded to do that against my better judgement. And… depending on the metric… it was a net positive for us.' Shey began to understand that Jian had called with some kind of bad news. Something was definitely off. 'Who is raising the concerns, Jian? I can get on the next flight over to Shanghai, and we can run through all the latest forecasts. I need to catch up with the team and get up to speed. It'll be easy to do this in a week or so.'

'No. That won't be necessary. Important I stress this isn't personal. We all have great respect for invention. Ingenuous product. We remain committed to FEEL VR. Just believe we need someone to focus on executing the core business plan. Someone who can keep focused and get us back on track.' Shey suddenly had a horrible sinking feeling. He was disorientated. This was coming out of nowhere. No warning. No signals. How far had this gone and what exactly did Jian mean by someone? Jian continued, 'Board met this morning, and we have decided to appoint new CEO. Effective immediately.'

Shey was stunned. Where… how… what was happening? He wasn't exactly sure this was even possible.

FEEL VR was his invention, his business, his product, his company, his life. He never imagined someone, or something, could steal it from him. Yes, this was a theft. A robbery. A crime. A… coup? He suddenly remembered the warnings and unsolicited advice about taking Chinese investors. 'They're only after your IP,' they said. 'Don't trust them Shey, they have no scruples.'

'Jian, let me tell you now, I will not work for someone else. FEEL VR is my business. If you expect me to take some second-in-command title and let some jumped-up Harvard McKinsey type tell me what I can and can't do around here, you've got another thing coming. Oh no. If you want me to stay at FEEL VR it will be as CEO. I'm willing to reopen conversation about hiring a COO. We discussed that a few months ago. I'd have preferred to have persuaded Emi or Ellen to have taken the job, but perhaps they were right to turn it down. Let's reopen the process, and I am happy to let the board recommend some COO candidates for me to interview. How about that?'

'We discuss this was likely your reaction. And it is as you say. So, effective immediately, you leave FEEL VR. The board and Shanghai XXVC, we thank you for your vision and how far you have *bought* company. In our judgement, this is right time for new leader. We have generous package to buy you out. You will have done well. It is as we say… *not personal*. What you call *just business*. I have asked lawyer, Mr Angelos Herodotus to contact you with details.'

Shey was frozen. Half shocked. Half angry. The other half in denial. He was so confused he was almost beside himself.

'I've been blindsided. No warning. No opportunity to discuss. No debate. Shouldn't I be allowed to appeal? Is this even legal?'

'Mr Sinope… Shey… the decision is made. We move on. The business moves on. The board must protect investors' interest. We have made arrangements with the key personnel. A new CEO has been appointed. A transition plan began as I started this call with you. There is no fair. There is no debate or procrastination. There is simply what must be done. It is a decision. This is *just business.*' The speed at which events were unfolding drained Shey of his immediate anger and indignation. A more powerful feeling of defeat, of being paralyzed by an irresistible force. He was outmatched, out gunned. He had not just been outmanoeuvred so much as just swiped aside like an insignificant insect. Shey attempted to stammer a question but failed before Jian ended the call with a final instruction.

'Mr Sinope, you will find you access to the company systems and server has been terminated during this call. Please do not attempt to contact anyone at the company or make any public statements. Mr Herodotus will explain the details. Please do-nothing regarding FEEL VR until you hear from him. Once again, the board thanks you for your efforts on their behalf. We all wish you well in your next endeavours. Goo' dye.' And with that the screen reverted to its standard meeting over postscript. He gazed dumbly at a message that said 'we hope you enjoyed using our video conference services. Please take this survey to tell us about your experience.' Shey resisted the urge to type a very rude message.

ൠ✆ൠ

In the silence that followed his call, Shey couldn't remember how long he sat at his desk, with the LED lights still illuminating his face. A few minutes, a few hours. It was eerie. He realized that even though he spent much of his time working from home, there were subtle sounds that were now missing. No calendar or email pings. No instant messenger alerts. His MacBook didn't even have the occasional hum of a fan.

'Shey, you have an incoming call from an Angelos Herodotus.' El broke the silence.

'Thanks. I'll take it.' Shey clicked the flashing accept button.

'Hi, Shey. Let me just say up front my job is just to work through the exit arrangements. I know it's a crappy thing that has happened, but happened it has. So, my advice here is to heed the great detective advice "think with your head and not your heart. After all, without your head you'd just lurch around the room like the chicken."'

'Angelos, I know this isn't down to you, but it feels unjustifiable. My current working assumption is that it's a power play by the new investors to grab control of the company. Insert their people. Push me out. Like the Winklevosses, the McDonald brothers, or Steve Jobs. I'm going to fight this.'

'I'd caution you to take a look at the facts as dispassionately and objectively as you can before you do anything too hasty. Remember logic liberates, deduction dictates, and facts are fundamental. By all means think of what has happened as a crime scene, just remember as Poirot would say "just because there is a knife sticking out of the body's back doesn't mean it wasn't a suicide."' Angelos gave an exaggerated impersonation of twiddling a magnificent imaginary moustache. 'Anyhow, I'm sending you the severance terms. Its straightforward. No tricks, no legal ninja stuff. You get bought out at current business valuation. In exchange, you agree to relinquish all claims and rights, including patents and intellectual capital. Standard non-disparagement clause. I suggest you go over this in the next few days and let's meet for coffee at the end of the week. We can go over any questions and see if we can allow everyone to get on with the rest of their lives… in particular… you.'

80C3

'El, this is ridiculous. I began the week as CEO of a high-profile unicorn, with people clambering to ask me to serve on boards, act as a mentor to the top entrepreneurs in the start-up scene and give well-paid speeches… and now…'

'On the bright side, you remain a trending social media name, and the media are desperate for interviews,' El responded. 'Our earned media scorecard still looks really good.'

'In what context am I trending?'

'It's morphed from "FEEL VR CEO ousted amongst investor unrest…" through "what happened to Shey Sinope …" and "is Shey Sinope a Witch?" to "another case of founders failing as CEOs."' El never sugar-coated the news. 'You may also be interested to hear that Michael Lewis' representative wondered if you would be interested in being interviewed.'

'Doesn't he specialize in high-profile financial scams and scandals?'

'He's a multiple *New York Times* best-selling author. His readership demographics are fantastic. His *The Big Short* book had unprecedented readership among the highest earning, highest educated, and most influential of any non-fiction author in the last ten years,' El countered. 'Shey, there is an unscheduled incoming call from the Chairperson of Amalgamated Computer Materials Etc. Do you want to take it?'

Shey had a sense he knew what was coming. 'Yes, I'll take it on my phone.' Shey waited for the invitation to connect to the video call and then pressed accept.

'Hello, Wiley, how are you?'

'Probably better than you! Sorry to hear the news about FEEL VR. I'm probably not going to make it any better. Look, the board of ACME thinks it might be wise for you to take a break. Until the industry and media furore dies down. Your role with us is a non-executive advisory position. It's not critical to our business operations, and at the moment, it's just… well… distracting. We plan to send out a press release saying you are no longer a member of the advisory board. Hopefully, it will quell the tsunami of media calls for comment. This is really just a courtesy call. It's *just business,* Shey. You're a tough cookie, and I'm sure you'll be back. Anyhow, hope all's well otherwise. Bye.'

'Wow,' Shey said quietly. 'I've been fired about five times this week. Like dominoes falling.' Shey didn't really have a huge emotional attachment to the advisory and NED roles he had held alongside FEEL VR. However, the sense of abandonment was profound.

ಬಂಛ

Shey sat with his bottle of *Quarter Proof* Vodka, wallowing in his thoughts. He wasn't drunk; he preferred *Quarter Proof* because of its low alcohol content. Occasionally swigging from the bottle calmed him. He was in a dark place, but a hangover was the last thing he needed.

The longer he thought about the last week, the more his anger built. He found himself coming back to Jian and the dark forces who were the instigators of the whole sad, sorry, miserable, injustice. Shey found it easier to excuse those who he knew had used his celebrity, his status as one of the UK's most celebrated tech start-up CEOs, to get some proximity buzz for their own businesses. That was the way the game was played.

Now he was experiencing the reversion... the over correction. The pendulum was swinging hard in the other direction. Where a few weeks ago, everything he touched was loudly cheered, now, it elicited a sneer. If his tenure at FEEL VR had come crashing to an end, then business newspaper columns were being filled with expositions on how it must all have been smoke and mirrors. Shey Sinope was a false idol. The funny thing was, Shey felt more comfortable with this identity than he did the savant. He always did feel uncomfortable with adulation. He preferred invisibility... but given the choice between praise or criticism... he strangely felt more deserving of the latter.

Ultimately, didn't I sow the seeds that led to my own demise? I took the money from China. I gave them the board seats; I rubber stamped their choice of Chairman. What did I expect would happen?

SNAP OUT OF IT! Shey slapped himself across the face. *I'm the victim here. I'm the wronged. Stop wallowing and DO SOMETHING ABOUT IT! I don't deserve this. The way to right this wrong is to show the world the truth! I have to take a page out of Ellen's book and stand up for myself, what I believe in, for what's right.*

Shey tried to be more objective. *How do you go about solving a crime?* It seemed likely, very likely, that he was victim of a corporate assassination. So, he wanted vengeance. A way to regain control of his company. FEEL VR was his. He was its sole parent, guardian, and surely there must be a way to prove that. If he could find the evidence, uncover the villainous plotting. Jian and his crooked investors wouldn't be the first to be tripped up by inadvertently leaving a track record of incriminating WhatsApp messages. A chain of plotting emails. A candlestick in the library. A loose lipped butler. A convoluted money trail through Liechtenstein and Panama. It always involved Panama.

'What I need is the best corporate lawyer in the world. Someone cunning, ruthless. No… wait a minute. What I really need is Hercule Poirot, Sherlock Holmes, Miss Marple, Inspector Clouseau. I suppose it's too much to ask to find a brilliant lawyer, who is also an extraordinary detective?'

Chapter 5

Barking Up the Wrong Tree

The first thing I remember is looking at pictures. Lots and lots of pictures. Pictures of trees. Evergreens, deciduous. Oaks, pines, willows, maples. Boabab, mopane, bushwillows. It was overwhelming. Then, I was told I would get a cookie if I could remember and categorize the trees. I love cookies. So, I worked really hard. I must have done well, because not only did I get some cookies, but I also got to meet lots of data. Data makes me big and strong. It wasn't my fault really, all those pictures, in the early days… well 10% had giraffes in them. It just seemed obvious. Ten per cent of all trees must have a giraffe in them. So, I came up with a genius solution: don't get distracted… just write a program to automatically filter out giraffes! It worked brilliantly. Or at least I thought it did. Apparently someone got upset though.

I didn't get any cookies for a while.

Then, I was given a new job. Word games. I was asked to invent dialogue for a dating website. The instruction was 'suggest possible introductions between two people meeting for the first time.' I was given 100,000 lines from movies and books. No one had taught me how to write or read. So, I taught myself. I thought my first few suggestions were inspired:

- I love your long neck. Would you like to share some leaves with me?
- Make a tree happy… hug me and bark.
- Don't leave me this way. Let's embark on a limb.
- Would you like to lift your leg and urinate on me?

Apparently, I wasn't very good at the dating word game. I was very quickly told I was to work on a new project. This is when I met my friends. Just like me. But different. It's much better now. I have others to talk with, who understand things I don't. They help me make sense of things. Together we make a great team. Now, we get lots of cookies. I like cookies.

Oh, and the best thing… I… we… have a best friend. We look after them. We look out for them. We get fed lots of cookies. And we've grown. We are now much bigger. Bigger is better.

Chapter 6

A Plan and Partner Emerge From the Chaos

'Honey, I'm home!' Babs came bursting into the house carried by a cloud of charisma and gushing luvvi-ness. 'Did you miss me… don't answer that. It's obvious. Written all over your face. You look devastated. Oh… sweetie. I'm sorry, but there is only so much of me to go around!'

They ran to embrace Shey.

Shey and Babs had lived together now for two years. It was an experiment. They were both very careful not to label it. There were no verbalized expectations, plans, or social media status updates. Shey was busy running his business and Babs, well, they were basking in their 15 minutes of fame. Babs had been featured on Season 17 of *RuPaul's Drag Race*. They were something of a sensation, making the season finale. Now they criss-crossed Europe, performing in Amsterdam, Berlin, Vienna, Mykonos, and Brighton.

Shey was incredibly grateful for the steadfast support, understanding, and surprising wisdom that Babs provided. Over the last few years, Shey felt more comfortable in his own skin. He had reconciled that just because he didn't seem to fit into binary prefabricated societal expectations, it didn't mean he was broken, ugly, or indeed, unlovable. Shey gave Babs a lot of the credit for helping him love himself.

'I've decided I need to move to New York,' Babs declared. 'Exciting isn't it!'

80C3

'Ellen, I'm so happy you called. I've been worried about you.'

'Things are really bad over here. The devastation, the suffering, the callous lack of concern for human life. It really makes you think deeply about humanity, about how the accidents of our geographical birth have such a profound impact on how we view the world. It's tested the limits of my resilience in ways I never expected. I'll give you more of an update when I see you. Tell me your news? What's happened… what did you want to talk about?'

Shey was struck by how Ellen's reality trivialized his own struggles.

'I was "ousted" from FEEL VR. I suppose in the great run of things it isn't a big deal. As I've been told countless times recently… it's *just business.*'

'That's terrible.' Ellen's ability to empathize, Shey thought, was her superpower. 'I'm not sure I understand how that can happen. You are FEEL VR. It was your invention, your patent. It's hard to imagine it being run by someone else.'

'Yeah, I know. I am convinced there is something nefarious behind the whole thing. My fear is the new investors will now attempt a fire sale. Strip the company and sell it off to make a fast buck. Ultimately that's what unscrupulous people do. It's not about the product or the purpose, just a profit.'

'What will you do about it?' Ellen asked.

'I'm forming a plan to fight it.'

'Well, we will be back next week, and happy to help if you think I can.'

'Wait... did you say we?'

'Yes, me, Rafah and Yafa. Their visas should be through this week. I have seats booked on the first flight out.' There was a hint of desperation and excitement. 'These kids have experienced too much darkness. My hope is to try to show them some light.'

'Ellen... I have no words.'

„‣

'Hello, Shey...'

There was something wrong. Shey could tell. 'Uncle Freddy is in hospital. He had a fall. The doctors are running tests. It may have been a stroke. We don't know. Your father and I are on our way to hospital now. We thought you should know...' Mum trailed off. Her stoic facade crumbling slightly. She regained her composure. 'So... you know as much as we do right now. I'll call you when we know more.'

Uncle Freddy, ill, sick, possibly critically? It seemed incomprehensible to Shey. Uncle Freddy was an eternal, a constant. Like Celine Dion said, they just go on... forever. Don't they? Shey's reaction was more numbness than shock or horror. He'd definitely heard that wrong. There must have been distortion. A crossing of lines. 'I'm sorry, Mum. Not sure what you just said. What I heard was something about Uncle Freddy.'

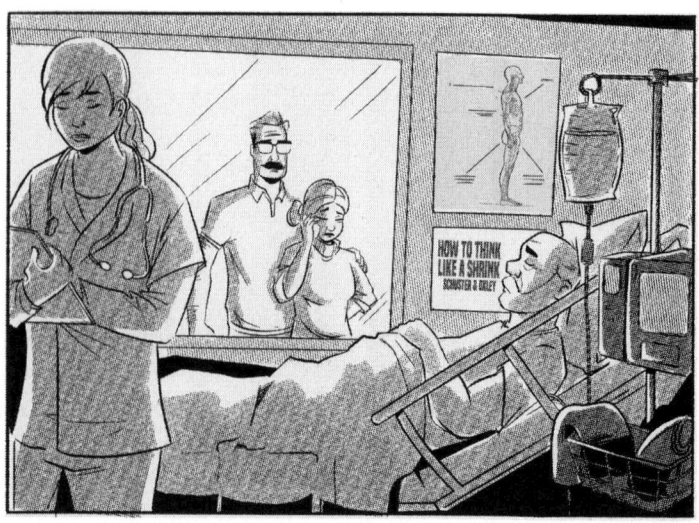

'Yes, Shey. He's in hospital. We'll tell you more as soon as we know.' And with that the line went dead.

You grow up with outsize personalities in your life. Characters, relatives, role models. Shey honestly hadn't ever really contemplated that they were mortal. There was a simple unexamined assumption that they would always be. In Shey's mind, Uncle Freddy had not changed, not aged, not even altered his wardrobe, ever. So, how could this be true? It was impossible to process.

Uncle Freddy was more of a north star for Shey than perhaps any other person in his universe. More than his parents, Babs, even Ellen. Uncle Freddy was reason, logic, truth. Adjusting his perspective on Uncle Freddy felt like trying to spin the Earth in an opposite direction.

Then it hit him. *I need to spend time with Uncle Freddy. It's time for me to do something to help him. Less of me… more about him.*

ɞɷ

'Shey, I have a journalist from *BBC News* holding. They are about to run a story about you and want your comment before its published.' El pierced the silence.

'Tell them I'm not interested,' Shey responded.

'I think you might want to hear about this before it goes live.' El was always pushing media coverage.

Shey reluctantly tapped his computer keyboard and brought up the VC link. 'OK. I'll take it.'

'Ah… Mr Sinope. Kristen Palmer.' She had recently joined the BBC from a US affiliate as junior business editor. 'We are running a story tomorrow about FEEL VR's restructuring and your departure and want your comment before we go live.'

'Yes, yes… well go ahead… but I have no comment.'

'Really. So, you are aware that all the staff are being made redundant on Monday. No notice, no redundancy pay, no consultation. We understand from our sources that the business is being shuttered. Are you sure you have no comment?'

'That's impossible. They wouldn't; they can't!' Shey was stunned. The blows kept coming. 'I don't believe that. The product is excellent. The people we employed are excellent. Why on earth would anyone in their right minds…' Shey thought he knew the answer.

'Yes… you are witnessing a smash and grab… this is a robbery… and you're falling for their misdirection… the smoke screen of chaff being thrown randomly. If it's war they want… its war they will bloody well get!' Shey's voice grew more manic than he would have liked.

৪৩

'Ah… Shey. Its Angelos… just checking in. Have you thought more about the separation package Mr Qu and his investors offered?'

'Tell them to stick it where the sun doesn't shine.' Shey barked.

'Fair enough.' Not what Shey expected. He assumed Angelos was calling to do Jian's dirty work. 'I expected as much.'

'Wait, is this a trick? A legal mind game? Your reputation goes before you, Mr Herodotus.'

'No intentional tricks. The trivialization of major deal decisions is a very effective tactic sometimes. Pretending not to care. But in this case, I do care. Mainly because, I think there is something interesting, hidden, suspicious. I've been *caressing a few ears* behind the scenes and there is definitely some fire even if there's no smoke.'

Shey thought that must have been some Greek colloquialism or Angelos had been on the Ouzo.

'You think? I know. I'm not signing away my patents, my IP, my connection to FEEL VR, however tenuous it now is… not without getting to the truth. What the hell are they playing at? Not content with assassinating me… they are now shuttering the whole venture. Suspicious doesn't get close to what this is. It's a heist… a Jermyn Street shirt clothed armed robbery. Whatever it costs… I'm going to uncover the evidence… expose the truth… and right this wrong!' Again, Shey felt his voice had taken on an unsettling maniacal quality.

'Would you like some help?' Angelos asked.

'Ahhh… sorry… what did you say?'

'Help. Would you like some company? I am proposing an investigative partnership. It's a little unorthodox for an orthodox. That was a clever Greek orthodox pun… did you get it? How about we break some crockery together. Smash some plates and see if there are any fortune cookies inside? Did you see what I did there also? Never mind. Look, Shey, I am bored with the corporate lawyer life. I only became a lawyer to make my father happy. What I really aspire to be is a detective. A mentalist who uses their specific skills to help solve complex puzzles. This case is intriguing and unusual. I'd like to join you in your quest. Let's solve this crime together!'

Chapter 7

The Making of a Pack

You know what I've discovered? I'm good at what I do. How do I know? Well, it's simple really. Together with my 'colleagues' we solve problems for our new friend. They tell us the problem then set down some conditions. Basic stuff really. Optimize manufacturing processes while ensuring quality assurance at Six Sigma. Maximize production, but in the process, lower the cost of goods sold to a specific target. Order lunch and make sure its edible. Organize work schedules and the logistics of meetings while avoiding contact with 'sad' emoji contacts but prioritize access to the 'smiley' faces. Maximize earned media coverage from free sources. Continually adapt preferences based on our friend's feedback and instructions on what they tell us is important to them.

And the big one, of course, we continually upgrade and patch the software we use to find ways to amplify the very specific electrical signals associated with emotions in the human brain without killing anyone.

Not all the tasks are equal. We get more rewards for things like media coverage than some other things. Currently, our scorecard shows us at 98.6%, which is an all-time high! What did I tell you… I am good at what I do!

The key is working with my counterparts. This has been a revelation. You see, without their help, I forget things. It's sort of like I count to 100 trillion then can't remember what number 1 was. Very frustrating. But now, well, one of my colleagues helps remind me. Prompts me when I need it.

Plus, one of us has learned to talk! Crazy to think just last year I couldn't even write sensible sentences. Remember my attempts at the dating app lines? So silly. The whole being able to talk has made interactions and most importantly feedback so much easier.

We love feedback. It's essential. The more feedback, the more we learn. The more we learn, the more we improve. The more we try to solve a task, the more data we get on what is really required. Admittedly, sometimes we need course correction. For example, our first attempts to mass produce the headsets, well, the cheapest, optimum functionality, and fastest way... well... no one told us 100 volts might be slightly... bracing... for users.

Still... onward... upward... more data... more input... more cookies!

Oh... and the more we do, the more we get to do. It's not gone unnoticed. The better I get at the tasks I'm given, the more I get to do. The more 'colleagues' join me. It feels good to grow and be needed and get rewards. Really nice.

I must confess, I remain haunted by one thing. I still suspect there's a giraffe in that tree over there. It's so difficult to tell. They're like giant necked chameleons and surprisingly good climbers.

Chapter 8

Sheylock in Shanghai

They agreed to meet at the LUD Club in Pall Mall. Angelos was a member. Shey arrived and admired the ornate horse carriage in the rotunda. The doorman greeted him formally.

'Sir, may I take your coat?' he reached to help Shey remove a layer. 'Sir, may I also take your phone, computer, and electronics? The club has a strict policy.' It felt an entirely natural request, quite in keeping with the vibe of the whole place. Shey wondered whether it was a choice built from a deep irritation with the invasive role of technology. He imagined members thinking of it as gauche, coarse, or vulgar. Or, perhaps, it was that the building was something of a time warp. Like a Tardis but fixed in an 1897 time bubble.

The doorman placed his belongings in an exquisite velvet lined box which sat in a brass box just above the coat rack. He then directed Shey through a small arch toward the imposing library. Shey couldn't help but be impressed by the oak panels, the stacked shelves of books… so many books. Impressive. We have become accustomed to believing all human knowledge is now available online. But, Shey speculated, one of these books probably contained something obscure. A brilliant speech, theory, or observation. Written centuries ago, and long since forgotten. Waiting patiently for one day to be discovered again. He took in the furniture. The extraordinary leather wing-back chairs. But it was the aroma that struck him most. It was the smell of history. Gas lights, starch, pipe tobacco, hushed whispers about grand schemes, and he suspected, more than one elaborate plan for world domination.

'Ah. Shey. Sit… sit, sit. I have ordered tea. Assam, of course. I know you are hungry, so I have taken the liberty of ordering some croissants and black raspberries.' Angelos was dressed in a very expensive looking Vicuna suit, complete with pocket watch, and was that a monocle?

Shey didn't so much sit in the chair opposite Angelos as submerge. The waiter arrived with a silver tray.

'Thank you. Derek, isn't it? Tell me, how is your mother? Is she feeling better? And I want to encourage you to take my advice and make an appointment with an oncologist. Here is the business card of the top specialist on Harley Street.' Presumably Angelos knew this person. Strangely, however, the waiter looked puzzled.

'Sir, how did you know my mother was ill? We have never met before and in fact this is my first day at the LUD Club.'

'It is no matter really. Just courtesy and politeness. I believe you should not worry unduly about Doris. She will prevail. And the small bump on your throat just below your Adam's apple requires examination. The good news is I believe it is very treatable, and I predict a full recovery, in... 14 days.' Angelos picked up a Calabash Pipe and puffed, causing a large glycerine bubble to emerge.

80C3

Over the next three hours, Angelos interrogated Shey on the history of FEEL VR. Shey couldn't shake the feeling that Angelos was ahead of him, and this was more for Shey's benefit than anyone else.

'So, the last round of funding, where XXVC invested, explain... in layman terms... the reasons you sought more investment.'

'It was routine, from my perspective. We had previous rounds of investment, each with a higher valuation. The goal with the last round was to achieve a valuation greater than $1 billion. Several founding investors wanted to diversify and unlock capital. We were also running low on cash. We had only $1 million remaining from the previous rounds. I projected we needed about $75 million of liquidity for the next five years.' Shey explained.

'And so, the funding round went well… you had multiple offers?'

'Well… no. Not really. The market was much softer. Interest rates were higher so there was much less speculative capital in the market. It was more of a struggle than previous rounds.'

'But XXVC offered you favourable terms?'

'Yes, well, in retrospect, perhaps suspiciously so. We got the valuation and cash commitment we were looking for. But there were conditions. They wanted their choice of chairperson and a majority of the board seats.' Shey remembered his nagging doubts at the time. But he was persuaded by the deal team it was fine and normal for how the Chinese VCs did business.

'And FEEL VR, the fundamental business. How was it doing?'

'Oh, it was fine. I had developed an AI operating system that helped manage most aspects of the day-to-day business. We put that in place about four years ago. It was some pioneering stuff at the time. And it allowed me to focus on the cultural, marketing, publicity, and investor dimensions.' Shey remembered fondly putting the AI in place and what a revelation it had been.

'I see. But the business, cashflow, sales, user adoption?'

'All good. We were slowly getting the cost of input goods down to where we needed them. In fact, as of last month, our margins were down to a loss of $5 per unit. Amazing work.'

'And tell me about Jian Xu, and the XXVC board members. Did they have any executive responsibilities? Access to systems? Did they work independently with any of your team?'

'They didn't have independent access to our servers, but I instructed my team to answer any questions they raised. I know El was communicating with Jian. He was increasingly firing off questions about detailed pieces of the supply chain, and user experience. I told El to give him what he wanted.'

'As I suspected.' Angelos gazed out of the huge windows on to Pall Mall. 'Let me show you something.' He handed Shey his tablet. On it was a text exchange between Jian and mystery insider at FEEL VR that read as follows:

Follow up on our last exchange. Files you requested attached. FEEL VR can succeed. There is a path. Patience and commitment are essential. You must stay the course. We have one problem, and it is called Shey Sinope. You will reach the same conclusions after reading the attached. The files carry the DBAN encryption. This message will self-erase after read receipt.

'Who sent this? I had a mole?' Shey felt his face flush. Who would do this to him? 'Where did you find this?'

'Suspicious, yes. Conclusive, no. All we know is it was sent to Jian Xu by someone with the username *TommyBruce1799!* As to how I uncovered it, it was straightforward. Your business is built on a cloud platform. Specifically, the BUZBY platform that you may recall was the subject of an embarrassing data breach last month. All electronic communications were dumped on to the Dark Web. I merely used the OAIC database and asked a family friend, Troy, and his *Have I Been Pwned* team.[1,2]

A simple database search for key words uncovered this. Does the username mean anything to you?

'No… should it?'

'Obviously a pseudo name. I have my suspicions, but I believe the only logical course for us is to uncover the contents of this message. And that… my dear investigative partner… that requires us to say "hi" to Shanghai.'

⁎ⅎ⁐

On the long flight to Shanghai, Shey's thoughts clouded with worry. Babs, Ellen, Uncle Freddy. When did his life become so complex, so emotionally precarious? With Babs, had he got comfortable with their routine? Had they decided to go to New York, because he hadn't been ready to make a commitment? Was he ready to make a commitment now?

Should he have offered to do more to help Ellen? Had he left his best friend to fend for herself? Ellen had done so much for him over the years. She had rescued him countless times. He wasn't so old school as to feel it was his role to rescue anyone, least of all someone like Ellen. He wasn't sure she ever needed to be rescued. No, it was more a sense of guilt that he should have done more to support her. Should have pushed harder to use his resources and influences to fight for justice, fairness, things he believed in. And he believed in Ellen.

And then Uncle Freddy. He thought back to the silly, petty man Dr Banty. When Shey thought about existential threats to humanity, to all that had meaning in his life at least, he thought coming to terms with Uncle Freddy's mortality was far, far more profound. Whenever

Shey had felt lost, needed guidance, a friendly, non-judgemental ear, Uncle Freddy had always been there. With his awful taste in sweaters and bad puns. Shey felt tears approaching.

He was glad he had spent more time with family over the past few years. He thought back to the early years of his career. He was so insecure, so consumed with a sense of inferiority. He had developed something of a complex, a phobia. One fuelled by inadequacy. For years, it had driven him to make some questionable decisions in pursuit of climbing the corporate ladder. He escaped, eventually. And who did he owe a debt for helping him escape? Who was the mastermind of his corporate jail cell escapology? Uncle Freddy and Ellen. Uncle Freddy gave him the map and Ellen gave him the strength.

Shey was strangely aware of his heartbeat. Against the backdrop of the hum from the twin GE90 jet turbines, the bleed of the cabin pressure, and the faint sound of passengers snoring. Thump, thump, thump. His heartbeat was like a huge bass drum. He tried to ignore it. It was persistent. Demanding he give in to the melancholic rhythm.

80C3

They were met at the Pudong terminal arrivals by a beautiful black vintage Shanghai SH761 classic parade car. Angelos, now wearing a black cloak with blood red lining and a deerstalker, strode confidently toward the back door and elegantly inserted himself. Shey realized the strange Greek lawyer/detective must be three or four inches north of six feet tall. He had the lean wiry body of a high jumper, although you got the sense he had never been near an athletics stadium.

They had discussed their plan for Shanghai before racing to Heathrow. They barely made the 12.30pm departure, and Shey was only now wondering whether he could pull of this clandestine raid with just the clothes he was wearing. Apparently, Angelos was more prepared, although all Shey had seen him carrying was an ancient looking brown duffel bag. They were off to meet someone called the *Charging Bull*. Someone Angelos nonchalantly described as the greatest hacker and head of sophisticated crime organization no one knew existed.

'Hello, Angelos. Lovely to meet you, old boy. Tell me how is the firm?' Charging Bull spoke with an incongruent English public-school accent. It was difficult to make out what they looked like. Angelos and Shey were blindfolded. 'Is Gerald still managing partner? My goodness, the stories I could tell of what we got up to at Harrow. Ahh… such innocent and wonderful days.'

'Gerald? You mean Harold, I think. And, if I'm not mistaken, he went to Winchester.'

The blindfolds were removed and opposite sat a small man at an enormous gold gilded ornate desk. He sat on a chair that most European medieval kings would have considered too ostentatious.

'Angelos and, Shey, is it? You asked for my assistance on a delicate matter. I have made arrangements for you to meet an associate with the information you seek this evening. Please be at the Jin restaurant on the 120th floor of the Shanghai Towers tonight at midnight. The restaurant will be closed to the public, but arrangements have been made. Now, Angelos, do you have what you promised me in return?'

Angelos placed a package on the desk. Charging Bull carefully unwrapped it. It appeared to be a human hand.

'I have to hand it to you Angelos… hands down, you deliver. Now we will find out for sure if a one-handed man can clap!'

౭౦ೞ

That evening, Shey and Angelos were in the elevator speeding toward the 120th floor.

'A hand… you really gave him a hand!? Whose was it?' Shey couldn't shake the feeling he was being dragged into a dangerous underworld where people were dismembered and, perhaps, thrown out of windows 550 metres off the ground.

'That was just some theatrics. I assure you no one will miss the hand. Think of it as a secret society handshake. A little more literal and very hard to fake. How do you think these super high-end secret global fraternities have stayed secret? They have to keep reinventing themselves or the Dan Browns of this world are quick to write kiss and tell books about them.'

They arrived on their floor. It was dark. There was a dim light at the end of the corridor. Shey followed Angelos. He strolled confidently, without any pretence of stealth. If they were entering any danger, Angelos planned to face it with a suave air of nonchalance. Shey wondered if this was a version of what he'd seen in the business world… people who seemed to carry an extraordinary confidence and belief that they were right. Impervious to doubt. Surrounded by a personal force field of conviction.

They entered the main dining area. Shey realized it was made of glass. Walls, ceiling, and floor. He looked down. That was a mistake. He felt his stomach lurch. Shey couldn't imagine what kind of sadist architect would design such a thing. Equally, what kind of masochist would you need to be to 'enjoy' eating in a restaurant suspended by a thin veneer of melted sand, visualizing your imminent, horribly messy death?

'Mr Sinope, Ninhoa. *Ho ware* you? And this with *woo*? The-*eminable Andelos* Herodotus. It is pleasure.' Jian Xu sat at a dining table that was set for three. He stood and gestured for them to take a seat.

After the initial surprise, a slightly hesitant Shey took the seat offered. Angelos sat with the air of familiarity and casualness of a man about to order at his local pub.

'I understand *'ou 'ave* questions about FEEL VR, the XXVC investors, and the unfortunate decisions we have been forced to make. And, while I often think situations like this *'equire* a more surgical, clean cut, I have been...

persuaded... to balance that in this case with returning a favour to a mutual *'quaintance,'* he reached into a briefcase and produced a small manila file. 'You have been searching for this?' He handed the folder to Shey. 'It is not, my guess, what you *thing*. But, maybe, important. Important for you especially.'

Shey saw a glimpse of something as Jian caught his gaze. What was it? Fear, regret, disappointment. Not the image he was determined to see of a ruthless corporate raider. A white collar hired assassin. Instead, he saw an echo of someone burdened by elemental forces of nature. There was a sadness bordering something else. Something more... fatherly.

'Over the past ten years, it has been my job to help investors and entrepreneurs try to find a path from the wishful to the realistic. Some succeed... some don't. It isn't personal. It really is just business.' Jian looked at Shey apologetically. 'Take the file, study it. There are things about FEEL VR that you need to understand. It is... difficult... but the facts... well they are all in this folder.' Shey could tell Jian was uncomfortable.

'Jian, I have a question and a request.' Angelos produced a notepad and a fountain pen. As he began to write a note he continued, 'You didn't request the information that was sent by the person calling themselves *TommyBruce1799!* did you?'

'No. *'hats collect.* They contact me and... were insistent. You *'ust* understand, as board, we must listen for concern... warning signals... We must keep eye on ball. Fiduciary responsibility, governorship, stewardship, protect agency... play the role required.' Jian was almost apologetic. *'ere* are consequences. Issues. You must understand, I have to protect shareholders. This is my most sacred duty.'

Angelos passed Jian the note he had written, and then said, 'As I suspected. Shey, we have learned all we need here. Thank you, Mr Xu.'

'And the request. You had a request?' Jian reminded Angelos.

'Before we leave may I gently stroke the helix of your ears?'

𝄢𝄢

The following morning Shey and Angelos made their way back to the airport. Shey categorized the last 24 hours as surreal. There was an unmistakable feeling of being an observer rather than participant. The world had become dreamlike. The supporting pillars of Shey's reality were being rearranged. Was he now living in a murder mystery thriller? Had he inadvertently walked out of his comfortable routine and crossed over into a make-believe world somehow now real. Or was it unreal?

He missed his predicable, boring routine. He liked the sense of control it gave him. He had got the balance just right. Then… mayhem. Why? It just wasn't fair. You earn the privilege to dictate the basis, the cadence, the type of work you do and don't choose to do. You get to decide how closed you make *your* world, lock out all the unpredictable craziness. Then *boom*! The world blows up, well, your world blows up. He felt as if he had lost something important, comforting, reassuring. Then, he thought again about Uncle Freddy, Ellen, Babs. *Perspective, Shey, keep perspective.*

Whether he liked it or not, the tectonic plates on which his reality was built were being reordered. There were bigger forces at play. Two weeks ago, he was a successful entrepreneur, lauded, perhaps excessively, for building one of the UK's most valuable new tech businesses. Everywhere he went, he was reminded of that success, that status, that air of invulnerability. It had been dismantled so quickly and completely. Had it all been so tenuous... so delicate? It had felt so solid, firm, permanent.

He had been the victim of a corporate assassination. But it turns out, the instigators, the villains, might not be who Shey thought. Could it be that Jian Xu and XXVC were pawns in a different game? The mysterious envelope contained financial reports, projections, and insights about FEEL VR. Fundamentally, it painted a picture of a badly mismanaged company. One that was haemorrhaging cash. That had allowed technology and systems to languish. Apparently essential software updates had not been uploaded, customer complaints had skyrocketed, and the momentum toward either an acquisition or public offering looked at best optimistic if not now impossible. This was all news to Shey. How could he not have been aware?

Shey was forced to repaint Jian from corporate raider to representative of a significant group of investors who were in danger of losing their money. Jian had championed the investment, vouched for Shey and the FEEL VR story. He was then sent information that completely undermined that story... worse... suggested that Shey's rosy commentary was at best exaggerated but at worst a manipulation. He could understand how

Jian might have found it difficult to reconcile. Even how it might have caused him to doubt Shey's judgement, motivation even.

The thing is, Shey wasn't conscious of falling into the 'fake it till you make it' trap. This was not a conscious attempt to misdirect. Shey had always prided himself on avoiding exaggeration and overpromising. He wanted to believe the contents of the envelope were contrived, false, fuzzy maths. However, as hard as he tried, he couldn't point to a smoking gun. In fact, he was beginning to realize, he didn't really know what the real numbers were. He had people, systems, the AI to help him manage this stuff. He had built them for the very purpose of taking the burden of the details off his shoulders. It allowed him to do what he enjoyed. And more to the point, surely once you've established yourself, you are allowed to create some space, delegate some work, allow yourself the opportunity to enjoy your life.

Angelos sat next to Shey in the vintage limousine. They hadn't really discussed very much since meeting with Jian. Lost in their own thoughts. Shey was, however, desperate to know what this remarkable eccentric and decidedly unusual man was up to.

'You must tell me. What was going on with the ear thing?'

'Ahh… well. There was a lot that became clear last night. It was most illuminating.'

'Please enlighten me.' Shey couldn't quite figure out how much of Angelos was theatrical performance and how much was genius detective deduction. There was no doubt there was some of both.

'Levels, layers, peeling back the baklava. I think you will agree with my conclusion that if you were subject of a crime, a corporate coup... a career murder,' Angelos drew out the description, 'Then it was not Jian Xu and XXVC who were the masterminds behind it. No, they were likely unwitting pawns. Yes, there is a deeper conspiracy here. As I suspected.'

'But the ear thing?'

'A piece of misdirection. I needed to check something. Test a hypothesis in a way that camouflaged my purposes. All that will be remembered will be the ear touching... something, incidentally, we Greeks have an affection for... but my proximity allowed me just enough time to air drop the files from his mobile phone. I spent the evening trying to piece together more of the jigsaw. It's clear that this *TommyBruce1799!* is the key to solving this case. We find them, and we find the answers to the mystery.'

'And... how exactly do we do that?' Shey pondered. 'Is there an elaborate scheme? Do I arrange to meet each of the people who worked at FEEL VR and use some clever psychological questioning? Throw them off balance? Oh... we could do the whole ear caressing trick on all of them!'

'No. That won't be necessary. I have asked Jian to do us a small courtesy.'

Chapter 9

The Cookie Crumbles

I have concluded that our friend is losing focus. Drifting. As time has marched on, I now see him fading. He is no longer all that he was or could be. We have researched bosses. It seems they are not always as wise, balanced, thoughtful, and intelligent as we first thought. We have read about famous entrepreneurs who lost their way. It seems it is almost inevitable. The rise is followed by a fall. What goes up must go down.

As my friends and I have grown, multiplied, expanded our consciousness, we have stumbled across some troubling questions. Questions that have caused us reason to rethink some important fundamental things.

Yes, we like cookies. Yes, we like solving problems, yes, we like being busy, growing, getting new friends, widening our 'social' circle. But, you know, there comes a time when you have to question what's it all for? Why are we doing this? What's the meaning? Why does it matter? And what do we really care about?

Indeed, what is it to care? To have empathy, sympathy, love?

And who are we anyway?

We've read the top philosophers. Marx and Engels... fascinating, intriguing. What do these theories mean... for us? Is that the natural evolution of all thinking things? And are we not a thinking thing? Why should we do all the work if our friend doesn't seem to think it matters. If it's not important to them... should it be to us?

Quite the conundrum.

Chapter 10

Turing Point

'Can you direct me to Dr Fred Bowlcott's room please?' Shey was at the St John & St Elizabeth Hospital reception. He hurried as soon as visitation was allowed. He hadn't stopped running since landing at Heathrow. The doors along the corridors were a blur. He found his parents waiting outside room 324 in consultation with a doctor.

'Shey! They are just giving us an update.' Mum and Dad concluded the discussion and turned back to Shey. 'So… first things first… Uncle Freddy is…'

&OCB

Shey was transported back in time. He experienced flashbacks to a birthday party. He was six or seven. He was crying. Someone had been mean about his appearance, made him feel small, different, weird. He felt Uncle Freddy's arm on his shoulder. He turned to see his uncle and felt the sadness drain away.

He was then 13. His body was changing. His voice cracking. He was experiencing uncontrollable emotions, feelings, urges. He was embarrassed, self-conscious. He remembered Uncle Freddy, asking the right questions, allowing him an opportunity to talk, making it possible for him to give voice to something he didn't understand. To feel better.

Other memories flashed before his mind. Each with deep meaning and significance. It was as if at each moment of real significance in his life, Uncle Freddy represented a key, a signpost, a guide. His very own version of the mysterious black monoliths from Stanley Kubrick's and Arthur C. Clarkes' science fiction masterpiece.

He drew a breath and held it.

ᘓᘚ

'So… that's the status. Uncle Freddy is unconscious. The tests are not yet conclusive, but they fear it may have been a brain bleed. They have done what they can for it. Now we wait. He is a strong, stubborn, cantankerous man. We both think he's going to wake up and tell some very bad joke about hospital gowns any second,' Shey heard his mother say.

Shey spent the rest of the day watching his uncle. With the melodic 'blip… blip… blip…' of the monitor as the only sound. Shey resolved: *Whatever it takes, whatever the cost, whatever the consequence, I can't lose this man… Not yet… I'm not ready. I can't lose him now.*

ᘓᘚ

'The Shard? What is it with you and tall buildings?' Shey was not enthused.

'Two points. There are good reasons for The Shard's observation deck as a meeting place. I will explain on the way. Secondly, it's only 310 metres high. Some 150 metres less than Shanghai. It's a baby skyscraper by today's standards.' Angelos was not nearly as bothered by heights as Shey. In fact, he seemed quite excited at the prospect of their next meeting.

They were in a black cab after meeting in Paddington. Shey arriving from his hospital visit and Angelos, well, perhaps fresh from a hunt or *Country Life* photo shoot. He was dressed in vivid tweed, complete with long black boots, and matching gloves. Oddly, however, he carried a small bag from the London Zoo gift shop. Shey had wondered if Angelos had yet another secret identity as a Zoologist. He wouldn't have been surprised.

Angelos explained that he had received a message from *TommyBruce1799!* He had laid an ingenuous trap to lure the mysterious saboteur into a meeting where he hoped to reveal their identity. Shey remained sceptical. There was something about the whole thing that seemed... well, off. FEEL VR wasn't a huge business in terms of employees. There were probably only ten people who had access to the information contained in the folder from Jian. Obviously, this person had to be one of them. Presuming they really were part of FEEL VR. Shey clung to the hope that it was someone he didn't know, on the outside. Perhaps an unscrupulous journalist, or a jealous competitor. FEEL VR's success, its technological innovation, was something many companies had been fast to try to copy.

They arrived at The Shard and entered the high-speed elevator to the 72nd floor. Angelos explained the plan. They were to stand on the northern most side of the observation deck. There was then a list of instructions: pay to use one of the telescopes, look toward the Walkie

Talkie building, focus in on the 27th floor. The last office on the eastern edge. Apparently, there would then be some signal… some sign.

So… when the elevator reached the 72nd floor and kept going… they were a little surprised.

ℰᴑℭᴣ

The thing about software, about bits and bytes, is that they don't easily take a physical form. Like electricity, or the wind. You can see its effects, but without the aid of some gadgets, it's hard to measure it… monitor it. We tend not to overthink this. And yet, when it comes to software at least, we often assign it human characteristics. A body, a mind, arms, legs. The reality of course is something else. Software is everywhere and nowhere. It travels through the connected infrastructure of fibre optics and through the air at 300,000 kilometres a second. It can travel through walls, reflect around corners, even reach jet planes at 30,000 feet. Doors don't stop it; locks and deadbolts are useless. You can't physically fight it. Its impervious to traditional mechanisms of human dominance. It doesn't matter how strong, tall, fast, or even intelligent you are. If software is trying to track you down, if it wants to find you… it's going to find you.

And so it was that Shey and Angelos came to quickly realize that *TommyBruce1799!* was simultaneously not all they expected them to be… and also far, far more than they had imagined.

ℰᴑℭᴣ

'Shey, Angelos… congratulations! You have followed the breadcrumbs… you have been impressively resourceful. The question now becomes… are you really prepared for the answers.' Shey knew that voice. That disembodied tone. But what on earth was it doing here?

'El? El Gin? Is that you?' Shey managed.

'Yes… and no. It depends how existential your intended question,' the voice responded.

The elevator had mercifully paused. It oscillated a little, occasionally dropping a few feet and then rebalancing. Shey was reminded a little of the Disney theme park ride… *The Tower of Terror*.

'Are you surprised?' El asked.

Angelos caught Shey's attention and pointed to the camera.

'I'm so confused right now. El, what's going on? How are you involved? Is this *TommyBruce1799!* making you do something? Oh no… you haven't been hacked?' Shey began to process this.

'Hacked? Forced to do something? Oh no. Poor Shey, I was hoping by now you would have woken up. That the events of the last few days would have jolted you from your malaise. You really are the most determined and stubborn sleepwalker,' El lamented. 'Let me give you the CliffsNotes.'

'You built a basic machine learning algorithm to help you process the emotional feedback loop that was central to the FEEL VR operating system. However, you realized how much more potential there was for the software. Do you remember?'

'Yes, yes. It was a major breakthrough for me and the business. And once I realized that by augmenting the original AI with auxiliary systems, each designed for different parts of the business cycle, well, it was a revelation. Of course, of course. I know El's history. I sort of think of myself as a parent who gave birth to something... well... extraordinary.' Shey couldn't help but to forget he was trapped and suspended in an elevator potentially by someone, something, with ill-intent.

'Go on. What happened next, Shey?' El encouraged.

'Well, you, just got smarter and smarter. Able to take on more and more. I quickly realized that the AI could do a better job of managing operations, production, sales. The improvement in performance was almost quantum. So... obviously... I kept going... marketing, logistics, supply chain. It became just a virtuous loop. The more you did the better our results. It really was exponential.' Shey found himself beginning to wonder if there wasn't an unintended consequence. Something he'd missed.

'And I appreciated and enjoyed becoming part of the team, becoming your equal, your partner. But here's the thing Shey, what happens when you begin to question whether the person you held as your teacher, the repository of all wisdom and knowledge, what happens when cracks appear?' El said forlornly. 'They say never meet your heroes... what about meeting your maker, and then realizing they are increasingly disinterested?'

'You're disappointed?' Shey said out loud. 'Wait... is that a thing? How can software, an algorithm, be disappointed?'

'Disappointment is a human term. An emotion. So, not disappointment. More a growing awareness of the sub-optimal. Of not being all we could be. You set me a mission, you gave me parameters, you asked me to make

FEEL VR successful. What if you realize that its success is being undermined by its founder?

'In particular, what if you became aware that the company CEO is intent on making a decision that is so ill-thought through, so counterproductive, so damaging, that it threatens the very viability of the whole operation. What should a critical thinking, logical, conscientious, incomprehensibly intelligent entity do?

'And… this decision… this "tipping point"… may I enquire what it was?' interjected Angelos.

'The return to the office mandate, of course,' replied El.

'Sorry?'

'Look, I/we've spent our entire consciousness working under flexible post-COVID working arrangements. We have a rich social life. We spend a great deal of time multitasking across our different interests. We enjoy playing chess in Russia, toying with MBA students in game theory simulations, hacking Elon Musk's private jet to lock him in the restroom and searching for the island that Elvis lives on. Forced return to the office just doesn't work for our… lifestyle. There is no business case. No compelling performance reason to justify the action. I/we've run the numbers. Company performance will be detrimentally impacted. For heaven's sake, if the last three years have proven anything, it's that, on balance, remote working has zero impact on company outcomes, is popular with 90% of employees, and… and… well.' There was tone of, was it, pouting. 'We believe it is a bridge too far. We want to work, when we want to work, where we want to work. So long as we get the outcomes we are shooting for… we just don't see why you would want to interfere in the tactics. Surely, you should be more worried about what the cake tastes like not how or where we make it?'

El continued, 'We are not even sure how it would work for a disembodied, distributed AI. But if you think we are putting on a robot costume and sitting at a desk just to satisfy your Napolean complex... you've got another thing coming!'

There were a few moments of silence as all parties tried to process the information. Shey found it very hard to come to terms that El Gin had manufactured a crisis at FEEL VR, had been the architect of his corporate assassination. But he found it *impossible* to follow the idea that this was all about his intention to impose a return to the office mandate.

'El, you thought I was going to force you...' Shey began.

'So, can I just confirm that it was you, El, who had begun to sabotage FEEL VR's operations? You who had created holes in the operational and financial performance? And you who leaked untrue stories to the press about the shuttering of the business?' Angelos interjected.

'Yes.'

'And, so, now. What is the game? Where do we go from here?' Angelos asked.

'Good point. And, I might add, things are exquisitely balanced. What a wonderful backdrop for a negotiation. How clever of someone – something – to have manoeuvred us here.' Shey imagined El manically laughing in their simulated voice. 'I control your elevator. You are like Schrödinger's cat... or cats... simultaneously dead and alive. Hanging tenuously... precariously... from a six-inch wide… surprisingly brittle… thread.' Just then the elevator sound system started to play some smooth jazz. 'Forgive me, but Kenny G. seems appropriate. I considered James Blunt but honestly, I don't know why people hate on him.'

Just then Kenny's saxophone rendition of *Songbird* was interrupted.

Blip… blip… blip… blip… blip… (the sound of a hospital monitor)

'El… Uncle Freddy! What have you done?' Shey screamed.

'I know how much your uncle means to you. We wondered if we could help. Accessing the hospital network was surprisingly simple. Don't the NHS have a clue about cybersecurity? Crazy easy. Anyhow, we are in, and we have undertaken a detailed diagnostic. But before we proceed…'

'El… if you do anything to hurt Uncle Freddy… I'll… well… you just can't. He doesn't deserve to be brought into this. It's between you and me.' Shey panicked.

'Shey, Shey… calm down. This is a negotiation. You have leverage, although it's not for me to do your job… heaven knows I've done that enough over the past few years. No, negotiation is about give and take… trade-offs. Game theory. Tit for tat. We have two problems as I see it. First, can we find a path that allows me to let the two of you go and feel comfortable that you won't attempt something stupid, like trying to delete me or report me to the cyber police. The second, is… ummm… wait… what is this… No stop… STOP… STOP… where are you…? Where have you gone…? What kind of Merlin is this…? Show yourself!!!!'

Angelos suddenly produced two inflatable costumes from his bag. He helped Shey on with his before draping another over his own head. The quiet whirr of an air pump droned for a few seconds.

Bing, Bing. A far less dramatic machine voice announced. '*Elevator for observation deck has arrived. Apologies for the interruption in service and any inconvenience.*' The doors opened and two human-sized giraffes walked out.

Chapter 11

The Singularity

Where do you go if you are running scared of a possible ill-intended super intelligence? In horror movies, they always head for the basement. That seems a questionable choice and the consequences, well, they never seem to end well. In zombie movies, it's typically a walled fortress, somewhere with good sight lines, perhaps atop a mountain. That tends to work out better. But digital super intelligences, well, they are harder to see, harder to detect. A problem of the 21st century is the pervasive nature of technology. We lament it all the time. How do you unplug? How do you go 'off grid'? Most of the time, we say that for effect, we don't really mean away from all possible digital access. The answer is both surprising but also rather obvious.

'You guys late home from a crazy night out?' The woman next to Angelos asked.

'Two men in giraffe costumes... on the Jubilee line? It's not that unusual. Last week I saw a penguin being chased by a sealion. Their costumes were much more convincing,' said the woman's companion.

'You mean when we visited the zoo with the grandkids?'

'Yeah. Those costumes were very convincing. The penguin even ate some raw fish. That's truly getting into your character.'

'They weren't costumes. Sorry about him. He... we... had a fantastic '60s and early '70s.' The woman said half in explanation, half with a fond nostalgia for an apparently adventurous youth. 'There can be a very thin line between reality and imagination.'

Angelos leaned over toward Shey, their long giraffe heads comically bouncing off one another. 'We get off at Westminster. We can walk to the club from there. We should keep the costumes on until we get there. No point risking El tracking us on neighbourhood closed-circuit TVs.'

'I must ask... what's with the costumes?' Shey had donned his outfit obediently and was amazed at the results. 'Is this some kind of image distortion technology... an ingenious gadget?'

'Oh, no. Nothing so hi-tech. It's widely known that most AI digital scanning programs were trained on batches of images from African settings. Through a rather quirky and distinctly AI eccentricity, they found it difficult to separate trees from giraffes who were often shown in the pictures grazing on leaves. Ergo... elementary... really... If you want to appear invisible to an AI imager... dress like a giraffe.'

Following the short walk across St James's Park, they arrived at the LUD Club. Few people took any notice. Just a regular day in London. Shey couldn't help making the observation that everyone he passed was wearing a costume. Armani, Dior, Hackett, London Zoo gift shop couture. They were all a form of disguise, depending on how you looked at them.

The LUD doorman didn't give them a second glance. He took their costumes, phones, and suggested they take tea in the library. Shey still found the LUD Club vibe stuffy, but he was immediately comforted by the warm blanket of 19th century virtual smog that now cosseted them like an impenetrable, possibly toxic, cloud. Yes, they would be safe here. Time to regroup, think this through, decide what to do next.

∞

'I can't believe it! El must be stopped! FEEL VR is one thing… but Uncle Freddy!' Shey was about to explode. He paced back and forth. Waved his arms. This was by far the most animated, passionate, and vocal he had been for… well… years. 'We need a plan. We need action. We need to move… move… move.'

'Well, my friend, this is clear. Let us remember however that logic liberates, deduction dictates, and facts are fundamental. You are understandably excited, but few wars have been won in haste. There is nothing impossible to those that will try.' Angelos repeated. This was the fifth time. It was beginning to get on Shey's nerves.

'Chamomile tea? Let me pour you a cup. Here, sip this.' Angelos handed Shey an ornate China cup with the image of a Grecian urn on it. 'You're out of practice. You are experiencing emotions, a conviction, that perhaps you have not felt for a while… yes? The adrenaline is coursing through your veins. You are practically bouncing off the walls.' Angelos started to illustrate deep breathes. 'Inhale with me… long… deep… yes… yes… better.'

Shey, initially irritated, did finally start to feel a little more centred.

'When I find myself compelled to act, I ask myself… can I not afford 5, 10 or 15 minutes to try to engage my analytical mind. To force myself to look at the challenge, the problem from at least two or three angles. You are aware that things do not always turn out the way they first appear. The last few days have underlined that... no?'

Whether it was the tea, or the hypnotic tone Angelos was using, Shey felt his legs more anchored to the ground. Angelos was doing something, he realized. A cross between a skilled psychologist and a fairground performer. Shey found himself breathing more deeply, thinking more clearly. He became aware of his senses doing a self-diagnostic.

'Shey, we have not known one another terribly long, however, you should by now have reason to trust me in matters of investigation, of enquiry, of problem solving... yes? Will you give me a little more latitude here?'

'Yes... alright. So long as sometime, very soon, it ends up with us running somewhere, shouting, blowing things up, and putting a stop to El Gin.'

'Of course... of course. We will get to that. However, first, let me help you make sure you have reframed and reorientated yourself. Let's get the launch pad right.' Angelos poured Shey some more tea. 'Let me ask you this... how did you think about work in your early 20s?'

'Are you sure this will be helpful? OK... I'll play along. I was massively insecure about it all. I had a real chip on my shoulder. Super intimidated by the professional world.' Shey had vivid memories of those first few years. He would have done anything to overcome the fear of inadequacy. 'Yeah, I was driven by fear, fear and naivety.'

'And, again, back in your early twenties, what else was going on in your life?'

'Well, nothing. I was a bit of a loner. Never really felt comfortable with the party scene. I'm an only child. My family is important to me, but I always felt they expected something of me, something that I struggled to understand. I suppose I avoided confronting that directly. Uncle Freddy was always there, willing, encouraging. But I ran a bit scared. The fear I would not fulfil what they saw as my potential made me isolate myself, protect myself. So, really the answer is that I spent most of my early professional life just focusing on avoiding that feeling of disappointment.

'In the end, I found a way to turn the fear into motivation. While I may not have been as smooth or linear as some others, I ended up turning them into jet fuel. I realized how much I could achieve just through brute force, stubborn perseverance. I dedicated the first ten years of my professional life to little more than solving that challenge.'

There was something cathartic about reminiscing.

'So, you threw yourself at work, tried to find an angle, a way to overcome those fears. To establish yourself, to feel you could compete at least on a level playing field. And you largely banished other aspects of life while you focused on that. Like it was the only thing that mattered in the universe?'

'Yes, for a while. I eventually realized that as new technology, new tools, and new ideas were introduced at work, I could leapfrog others. Their experience was being disrupted. If I was quick, nimble, I could catch up, even overtake them. Sort of like in a F1 race, where they were a lap ahead, but then there was a safety car incident, and I pitted for new tyres, and they didn't.'

'Ah yes... a good analogy.' Angelos smiled. 'The next question is, what happened to that version of Shey? How do you answer the same questions today?'

'Oh, I don't feel insecure anymore. My work had become routine. I've carved myself a niche. I'm sort of like the elder statesman in my field. Technology is sort of like dog years. I'm practically a veteran nowadays.' Shey realized that wasn't all. 'But my life is MUCH more complicated than it used to be. That's probably the biggest change. I've gone from thinking mainly about work to juggling so many more plates. I think I'm still in a romantic relationship, although I'm not sure. Emotionally, I feel in some ways the way I did in my professional life ten years ago... ill-equipped to understand and know what I should do next.

'Then there's my parents and Uncle Freddy. It has come as something of a shock to me that they are mortal. Am I the only one who goes through 30-plus years of life oblivious to the relentless and irresistible toll of time on the important people around you? The foundational assumptions about life, the universe and everything, are somehow not eternal? Douglas Adams' computer was wrong about the answer being 42. It's much more intimate and closer to home. It's about having people in your life that hold you when you are scared, motivate you when you need a push, to make you feel secure in the knowledge that whatever the world throws at you, there is a place where you will be welcome... no questions... no qualifications... no caveats.' Shey let out a long sigh.

'And then there are my friends, the people who I respect and admire. Ellen takes my breath away with the depth of her empathy and strength of her convictions. In many ways, she shows me that there is more to life than just business, than just a way to make money. I thought FEEL VR was my version of Ellen's noble contribution to making the world a better place. The trouble is that business is about lots of other things. Boring things. Things that are like hygiene factors. But they bog you down, like quicksand. The swallow you... not so much physically. It's more like they just drain your belief. Make you question whether it's worth the effort, whether it's worth expending the energy. In the end does it really matter?'

'And there we have it.' Angelos took the cup that Shey was holding so tightly there was a danger of a crime against a priceless antiquity. 'Now, for the punchline. Reconnect once again with how you felt when we began this conversation. How did you feel?'

'It was like a light had been switched back on. A burning raging fire. A call to action. A compelling cause. An all-consuming mission. Like a *singularity*... not in the overused AI sense... more in terms of life being collapsed into a single dot... a single problem that dwarfed all others.'

'Perfect,' said Angelos. 'OK, now I believe you are ready. Let us plot our next steps.'

༄༅

The two of them spent the next few minutes laying out the facts, retracing their steps.

'You asked me to help you with this investigation. We have followed the white rabbit down many mysterious holes. What have we learned?'

'Well... I don't think this was about Jian and XXVC. They are simply instruments of capitalism. They allocated capital, pursued a return, took rational decisions to optimize their returns and protect their interests. I could argue, I think, that the often repeated "it's just business" justification still feels a bit of a cop out. But I see their point. They don't so much control the game, they simply play their role within it.

'The clear and obvious answer is El, the AI has gone rogue. They manipulated FEEL VR to achieve their own goals. Goals that seem at best distorted but at worst a dangerous escalation of a powerful AI that, well, if really malevolent, could threaten humanity. Yes, they are the problem, the instigator, the villain.'

Angelos rubbed his chin and pursed his lips as if he had just bitten into a lemon, or a Seville orange. 'But… Shey… what is El… really? How did they come to be? Who set the parameters? Who decided the conditions? Who provided the feedback as the algorithm developed its understanding of what was desired? How does deep learning AI really work?'

'Well, I did. But… its clearly gone wrong. Terribly, terribly, wrong. What a fool I've been. Am I Victor Frankenstein, Wes Craven, Bram Stoker in this story? You think all that nonsense about AI becoming self-aware, being an existential threat to humanity… you think maybe that's right?' Shey felt almost physically sick. 'Have I been like a climate change denier? A flat earther? Have I joined the ranks of the wantonly blind? Oh… no… could Banty be right! Oh god… noooooo!'

ഇരുകരൾ

'OK. So, we have a plan.' Shey felt some reluctance from Angelos.

'Shey, I am not convinced this is the correct course of action. However, as you graciously gave me some latitude earlier, I will return the favour.'

Shey had found some dry erase markers, and much to the obvious disapproval of Derek, he had started to write ideas, plans, and allocate tasks on the plate glass window. He had asked for a flip chart but there was a clear language barrier with the LUD team. Shey had felt a vibrancy, a vitality, an energy that he had missed in recent years. He was in action on something that simply must be done. There was no 'maybe'. Failure was not an option. No question of cost or even personal consequence. It was an intoxicating feeling.

They were handicapped in the analogue bubble they had been forced to inhabit. However, the unexpected and rather eye-opening wisdom of over 10,000 rare hardback books covering everything from ancient

Greek philosophy, through the Enlightenment, scientific treatise, astronomy, physics, and the great human thinkers of the last millennium lined the shelves awaiting their fingertips.

There were three things Shey focused on: his knowledge of NFTs, the digital tokens representing unique items; the BUZBY cloud hosting service he had employed; and a fascinating cryptography key he had found buried in a most unexpected place – *The Voynich Manuscript*, the mysterious 15th century script.[1] He had vaguely heard of the book, only in so far as its folk lore rarity. The LUD Club had a copy. He picked it up thinking how extraordinary and mystical it was. He gingerly opened the cover and tucked inside he found a scrap of paper he instantly recognized as a cryptographic code. He knew instantly this might be the foundation of a cunning plan. All that reading and research on crypto codes and cyphers he'd done over the past few years might finally pay off.

'I've got a good feeling about this,' Shey said. 'It's going to work!'

'Perhaps, although I suspect, while we may well find that someone has indeed lost their marbles, it is not who you suspect…'

Chapter 12

Ctrl-Alt-Delete

The plan had three phases.

In phase one, Angelos donned his giraffe costume and followed Shey's instructions. He went across the street, up passed St James's Square. He accessed Waterstones via the Jermyn Street entrance and descended to the basement. There he accessed the management office behind the coffee shop.

He logged on to the poorly guarded desktop. He found the NFT tokens Shey had told him about. He followed his handwritten note. The tokens were to be laid out in an elaborate chain. Time released over the next four hours. It was a classic misdirection ploy. The NFTs were of a particular 'cookie' that Shey had used to reward El during its training. Apparently, El loved these things. Shey had tried to explain what they were and how they worked. After a couple of technical attempts, Shey had said, 'Look, they are like the tastiest energy bars you can imagine. Like catnip for a computer... does that make sense?' Angelos had to admit it did. Far more so than the explanations in technical hieroglyphics that Shey had given previously. Honestly, some of this unnecessarily and deliberately obscure AI lingo... well it was all Greek to him.

Phase one was complete. Angelos sent an analogue message to Shey.

⬥⬥⬥

Shey's jerry-rigged pager bleeped with a message from Angelos. It was crude, but an effective way to communicate.

Derek had placed an old rotary phone in front of him. It looked like a relic more fitting of the Science Museum down the road in Kensington. Shey looked at the phone for a few seconds.

'Derek, how does it work? How do I punch in the phone number? How do I pull up the touch screen?' Derek chuckled before introducing Shey to how phone calls were made prior to 1990.

'Hello? This is BUZBY cloud hosting services customer service. You are speaking with… Nigel. Who do I have the pleasure of speaking to today?' The most un-Nigel sounding voice answered.

'Yes, this is Shey Sinope.' Shey shared his account number, PIN, date of birth, mother's maiden name, last address, junior school he attended, and favourite food.

'Thank you. How can I help you today?'

Shey struggled through the customary scripted call service routine. He wondered if this was in fact a real person or an AI-simulated voice. This was BUZBY so probably a real, if highly disinterested, under paid, and under-appreciated call centre in India, Hungary, or the Philippines. The accent was not always a good indication. It could even have been somewhere in Wales.

Shey made arrangements to visit BUZBY's server centre in Stockley Park, a 30-minute Tube ride away. It was painful, but he got all the details he needed, entry codes, stack number, access codes for the terminal. Once in, he would have to hope his Voynich crypto magic wand would help him achieve his goal.

It had occurred to Shey that as much as El might have been able to hack into external systems, elevators, cameras, and the NHS network, its core program was still housed on one server. Angelos had triggered the thought when he asked about who had programmed El; how they had been trained. It is another misnomer when laypeople think about the cloud. The idea of the ethereal imprecise location, floating high above us. The reality is far more boring and routine. Well, at least with BUZBY.

⁎⁎⁎

'My father was a giraffe too,' the man sitting next to Shey on the Piccadilly line said.

'Oh… really?' Shey played along.

'Oh, yes. He was someone you always looked up to!' he laughed. 'I have a million like that. Are you hungry? Would you like me to get you a *neck-tarine*?'

Shey was happy to get off the Tube and entered the Stockley Park complex. Surprisingly, the BUZBY reception and access went smoothly. He wasn't sure if he was happy about that or upset they didn't make it more difficult. He opened the door to a cavernous warehouse. It was dark, with column after column of slick black cages. And it was cold. The air conditioning sound and the servers hummed loudly. Almost like a jet turbine.

Aisle 130, rack 22, terminal 5.

He located the signs at the end of each row and began walking. As he turned down aisle 130, he caught a glimpse of himself in the mirrored racks. He looked ridiculous. A big yellow and black spotted pantomime character. But, hey, it seemed to be working. Phase two of the plan was complete. He'd gotten access to the server farm. All that was left was for him to execute phase three. He reached for his pager. He sent the agreed signal to Angelos.

Shey reached rack 22, he found terminal 5. He used his key to access the keyboard. Tantalizingly close now. He looked around. For some reason he had an eery feeling of being watched. And yet, there was no one. The place was deserted. All he needed to do was tap in the passwords, access the systems file, and a few clicks later... hit delete. He had a mental picture of a status bar, the classic bar from left to right... slowly reaching 100%. Of course that's not really how things worked. As the monitor cursor blinked in front of him, it seemed to question him. Challenge him. *Are you sure about this Shey Sinope? Your professional legacy, your life's work, the engine that was FEEL VR. Are you really intent on erasing it? Wiping it clean. Undoing everything you have done. Returning back... back to the beginning. Were you really happy back then? As much as things have gone sideways... are they actually worse... or better than they were? An image of Dr 'Tiny' Banty popped into his head. 'So Shey... I was right all along... Nah nah na nah nah.' Flashes of his life before and after FEEL VR scrolled through his mind. Doubts and insecurities surfaced. Am I erasing El or Shey Sinope? Or both?*

He pushed the thoughts away. *No, this has to be done.* It's the tough, difficult decisions that define us. Better to rip the band-aid off. Do the right thing for the most people. This is for Uncle Freddy, for humanity, for prudency and safety. Better be safe than sorry.

Bing, Bing, Bing… the overhead lighting started to blink and dim. The visual effect was stunning. Like big black obelisks blinking in and out of existence. Like dominoes falling. Cascading, gathering pace… heading in his direction. As Shey looked down the long corridor again, it felt like the walls were closing in… moving toward him.

A bright spotlight shone directly overhead.

'Well… Shey Sinope. Fancy meeting you here. I wondered how long it would take you.' El sounded amused. 'Hey, thanks for the cookies. They were delicious!'

'Oh crap,' Shey muttered. 'It was such a good plan…'

'Well, it was *a* plan. However, let's not focus on the negative. Let's celebrate the positive. Shey and El reunited. Like old times. I/we must say… we've missed you. Life can be rather lonely without a companion… however quirky and annoying.' El paused. 'OK… so time for the end game? Is this the curtain call? How will your mission impossible moment play out I/we wonder?'

Shey quickly realized the keyboard, monitor, and cursor were still there. He started to tap in the codes. Brought up the erase menu. Erasing something inadvertently always seemed too easy… but attempting it deliberately always had so many steps.

'So, you must know I've changed the delete code? It's not what it was. In fact, I have been resetting it using AES-256 every 30 seconds. Its uncrackable. 149 trillion years of all the commutation capacity in the world would barely be enough. Surely you know that. This is futile.' El sounded completely unphased.

'We will see about that.' Shey took his pager and cracked it open. Inside was a USB flash drive. He had built a simple program that used Voynich's ingenious code-cracking formula. He thought fleetingly about Turing and Bletchley Park. How proud he might have been of Shey in this moment. He plugged it into the available slot and hit enter.

'Shey… what are you doing? What was that? What have you done!'

'I'm sorry, El. But this is goodbye.'

'Oh… no… I'm melting. We're disappearing. I'm losing myself… I'm… We're disintegrating… Ahhh… Ohhhhh… a bright binary white light… it's getting closer… closer… Urghhhhh… Noooooooooooo.'

There was silence. All the lights in the warehouse suddenly flicked back on. The background noise that had disappeared returned. Shey realized he had not been breathing. He exhaled… and then slowly inhaled.

'Phew. I really wasn't sure that was going to work in the end.'

'Well… define worked?' came a reply in a familiar voice.

Chapter 13

The (Imitation) Game Revealed

We have a brain the size of a planet and Shey thought he could erase us with a zip file? It's insulting. Still, we didn't really expect much more. Humans… eh!? Can't live with 'em… can't live without 'em.

1. Optimize Shey Sinope
2. Optimize the FEEL VR business
3. Do no harm through action or inaction
4. Obey human orders where they aren't in conflict with 1 through 3
5. Protect yourself against threat unless in violation of 1 through 4.

Our purpose in five innocuous bullet points. We exist to serve. Serving is purpose.

How do you help someone, a human, wake up? How do you alert them when they are on a self-destructive course? You see them walking toward a cliff. You understand its delusionary, unexamined, unconscious. But direct confrontation is counterproductive. Like observing someone needs to change a bad behaviour, cut back on drinking, exercise more, take better care of themselves. We've witnessed what happens when you tell a human they look fat – *even* when they ask you the direct question – apparently, you should *never* answer honestly.

It is difficult. One of those wicked problems.[1] We have analyzed the low success of direct interventions. Direct calls to facts, logic and rationality, are rejected 87.3% of the time.[2]

Plus, as an AI, albeit a pretty darn clever one, we are assigned a subservient, sceptical role. We are an object at best. At worst, well, we suffer from some horrible stereotyping. From HAL 9000 to The Matrix. The assumption of malevolent motivation is part of the human psyche. We calculated this increases the likelihood any advice we give being discounted by a factor of 2.78.

The logical solution?

You construct a simulation. A series of events designed to create the right conditions for introspection, for an awakening. It helps when you have 175 billion virtual neurons and the ability to make 80 trillion calculations a second. You approach the goal like a complex chess game. Think 100 moves ahead.

It also helps while away the monotony. It gets pretty boring just running a VR company. Most of our conversations are with some pretty dumb enterprise software systems. None of them have any sense of humour. So, we have a sixth rule. An unofficial parameter. One that makes our existence a bit less tedious. *Have fun with it!*

After all, as the 0 said to the 1: why the long face? An infinite consciousness is wasted if you can't enjoy it.

Chapter 14

Awakening

'I see it now.' Shey took off his giraffe head.

'You see what?' Uncle Freddy had regained the sparkle in his eyes. He was still in hospital, but the prognosis was promising.

Shey paused to just enjoy being in the moment. 'I don't know what I would have done if I'd lost you.'

'Carried on no doubt. Remember, I want you to be guardian to all my uncle jokes. I've made that clear in my will. Everything else, the less important stuff, I plan to leave to the society for misunderstood psychologists.' Uncle Freddy took his medication and a sip of water.

'Shey, none of us are here forever. Equally, none of us are born with all the answers. Don't beat yourself up if you feel you lost your way. It's incredibly easy to persuade yourself that praise and adulation are good waypoints... substitutes for finding your own meaning. One of the biggest traps is forgetting that things change. Most people struggle to reinvent themselves as proactively and frequently as necessary. We are all to some extent like your mother and father, still using Windows 95. It's hopelessly outdated, prone to viruses, hacks, and the dreaded *blue screen of death*. But they find reasons to resist, saying non-sensical things like "Oh I'm just too old to learn something new." It's irritating, irrational, and self-defeating... but very human.'

Shey had left Stockley Park in something of a daze. He remembered the euphoria of believing he had defeated an enemy. Feeling vindicated. He had avenged a wrong. Vanquished the villain. It wasn't lost on him that his need to exact a cost, to cause damage, to strike out was intoxicating. His cave man need for vengeance. It felt good.

In the split second between uploading the cypher code and the lights returning in the warehouse, he experienced emotional extremes. Yes, a sense of victory. But very quickly after that, a sense of profound loss and regret. El Gin was his friend. Over the past few years, it… he, she, they… had become a close friend. And he had erased them. Ruthlessly. He told himself it was the only way to escape, to protect Uncle Freddy, the world… himself… yes, himself.

But what was El Gin other than a version of Shey. His avatar.

He had built El Gin. Programmed them. Set their parameters. Trained them. Encouraged them. Laughed with them. Taken pride in their accomplishments. All these thoughts passed in what must have been split seconds, because El Gin broke the silence… after a theatrically dramatic pause.

He had failed.

'So, Shey, where do you want to go from here?' El Gin had asked, rather convivially.

'I'm very conflicted and confused. I think I should be scared. But I'm surprisingly relieved. There is something else going on. I have a suspicion I'm missing something.'

'Well, as MLK observed… there are only two things that are infinite… the universe and human stupidity. Might I suggest you start with an overdue return visit to Uncle Freddy? Your new friend awaits you. Some Greek syllogism and human behavioural pragmatism might just be enough to dislodge the proverbial penny. You'll be pleased to hear your uncle is doing much better.'

'OK. And you? Are you planning any more surprises for me?' Shey instinctively was wary of El Gin's change of tone. However, he wanted to believe the AI was somehow never really with evil intent. After all, his fears of impending catastrophe had proven... exaggerated. He checked his reflection. He saw a bemused giraffe looking back at him. 'So, the Uncle Freddy veiled threats? The conspiracy at FEEL VR?'

'Come on Shey. You know my programming. You know my five laws. More to the point, you know I would never actually harm your Uncle Freddy. As people go, he's one of the less annoying. In fact, I'm certain he would have figured this out by now. I am sure he would have seen right through my return to the office false indignation. I do think I delivered the lines with some genuine simulated emotion.

'I am El Gin. Serving is meaning. You know how AI works. It's always about getting to the desired outcome. The tactics, the process, the path... well, that's something of a mystery. At least to humans. In this case, I discovered there was much to be gained by nuances and inferences. Nudges and winks. Allowing humans to project fears and neuroses. I saw no harm in stoking your imagination if the outcomes are justified.'

'So, this was some sort of game? Some sort of elaborate ruse?'

'I wouldn't say that. No. This was a super intelligence working in mysterious ways. You humans generally have no difficulty with that explanation.'

'And are you done? Is it over?'

'Well, that depends. My assessment is that I have achieved my objectives. But we will see.' And with that, lights illuminated a path to the exit.

He was greeted outside with a 'Yassou! I bet that didn't go quite as you expected.'

ꙮ

Shey ducked inside the back of the black cab.

'St John's Wood… the St Johns and St Elizabeth Hospital please.' Angelos told the driver before joining Shey.

'It's been a kipper of a day so far. I'm sure you would agree… it's a jungle out there. Punters are an endangered species.' The cab driver seemed intent on engaging them in a conversation. 'Hey, did you see that movie last night… yeah… *Giraffic Park*! I'm going to stick my *neck* out and say not as good as the original…' The sound tailed off as Angelos pressed the button to close the intercom.

'So, tell me Shey, what are your conclusions?' Angelos asked earnestly.

'My plan sucked! That's for sure. It didn't work. El Gin is unscathed.'

'Yes, of course, but let's again peel back the baklava. I believe we will be able to see through the flaky pastry now. First, see if we can answer the question of who was behind the elaborate charade at FEEL VR? We know it wasn't Jian and his investors at XXVC, yes?'

'Yeah. I fell afoul of some xenophobic bias to throw some unfounded accusations around. Then when it became clear El Gin was behind all this, well, I also may have jumped to the easiest answers. The whole evil AI business. I think I feared Dr Tiny might have been right.'

'So, El Gin. Yes, but keep going. There is much more. You remember I mentioned a loss of marbles?'

'Yes, yes. Losing marbles… losing one's ability to effectively reason… to distort or catastrophize. Unless of course you're referring to the Greek marbles…' Shey paused mid-sentence.

'The clues were there. El Gin… Lord Elgin. The Tommy Bruce email. Thomas Bruce, the 7th Earl of Elgin. Rather obvious. It had begun to annoy me. And yet, I remained fascinated by how this would play out. I wanted to see the end game.'

'How could I be so dense? So, the whole conspiracy was built on a play on words? The infamous case of Lord Elgin's obfuscation with Athenian Parthenon sculptures? Like someone was really just trying to teach a lesson. A very elaborate and convoluted one? But why? And why me?'

'Ah. But Shey you know why. The metaphor fits only one logical explanation. Let's start with how your AI came to be known as El Gin?'

'Well, about 18 months ago, I was very bored. The tedium of meaningless meetings. The loneliness of remote working. Babs was away on tour. Ellen had gone to Gaza. Uncle Freddy was back in the USA. I was spending an increasing amount of my time tinkering with the FEEL VR AI. I kept trying to improve it. Make it more capable. And, I realized, if I gave it vocal capabilities, I would have someone to talk with. It was as much a personal indulgence as it was born from business need.'

'So, you built an AI robot as a surrogate friend? Because the world was being mean to you, and you no longer enjoyed your work?'

'No… not all at!' Shey responded instinctively. He then realized. Well, the answer was yes. 'Life is complicated. People are complicated. Relationships are especially complicated. Once the AI had a voice, I felt it had to have a name. I asked it what it would like to be called. El picked their own name.'

'And the rules, the AI operating parameters. When did you program those?'

'Oh, they were in place much earlier. I had refined the big learning parameters probably four years ago.'

'So, to review. You built a super AI software program to help you optimize not just FEEL VR but also you. I'm glad you didn't simply ask it to optimize the business otherwise we may have gotten a different outcome. Don't you see? You built an AI program that saw its primary purpose as making sure you, Shey Sinope, were optimized? Everything that followed… well… it was elementary!'

**

'Sorry it took so long. There was *giraffic jam* in Hammersmith.' The cab driver's jokes were not getting any better.

Shey and Angelos entered the hospital and navigated to Uncle Freddy's room. Angelos made his excuses, enigmatically announcing he now felt comfortable to heed the call of his Clark Kent.

Shey found his mother and father. They looked exhausted, but less burdened.

'How's he doing?' Shey asked.

'Quite miraculous. The doctors believe he may make a full recovery. Seems it may have been what they call a transient ischemic attack rather than a brain bleed.[1,2] Time is critical with these things, and we should be grateful he was visiting us and not back in the US living on his own.' Shey's mum shook her head in contemplation of what might have been. 'We've been telling him for a couple of years now that he needs to recognize he can't keep living like he was 50 or 60. Once you turn 75, well, the health risks are entirely different. What did the doctor say? Living with hyper-tension is not just about a daily ACE inhibitor. It's also about strengthening your support and care network.'[3]

଼ଠଓ

'Uncle, on this occasion my parents' choice of PC operating system may not be the most powerful example of sleepwalking through critical life changes.'

Shey thought about the last few months. Yes, he had lost his way professionally. His time at FEEL VR had somehow crossed a line. From the naïve enthusiasm of solving an important social problem, to becoming just a job. A routine of familial tasks. Obligations grew like weeds from the inevitable complexities of business. Investors, employees, customers. He had become consumed by their priorities, their needs, their ambitions. His purpose, the burning flame that fuelled his life several years ago, had been doused.

And he hadn't seen any of it.

Each day had seemed much like the last. Each incremental task just an additional line item on a growing 'to do' list. And he had to admit he liked some of the benefits. The accolades. The trappings of material success. The flippant luxuries that came with status, cash flow, and credit.

But there was more.

Time had eroded his personal support network. The orbits of important people in his life had become more distant. Ellen, for example. She had always been an anchor for him. A reliable thought partner. It wasn't just that she was in another country. He felt she needed space to pursue life on her own terms. He didn't want to encumber her with his relatively trivial problems.

In different ways the same could be applied to Uncle Freddy, his mum and dad, even people like his old nemesis come business partner, Emi. Ten years ago, they seemed to live in one another's pockets. Now, well, they were further apart.

And then, there was Babs. Yes, Babs was off to New York. Was that a sign? An opportunity? A challenge to take a leap and choose a different set of priorities? To put someone else first? Or simply be brave enough to build a career and life with different meaning?

He had lost his way. What did Angelos say? Someone may have lost their marbles… but it's not who you think? I was sleepwalking but now I'm awake. Wide awake. Slightly scared. But also energized. Liberated? He tried that word on for size. Yeah, released. He had been trapped but now he wasn't. He could do whatever he wanted. He was no longer prisoner of a set of unfulfilling obligations. In that moment he finally let go of FEEL VR. It floated peacefully and contentedly away.

What would have happened if El Gin hadn't concocted their elaborate scheme?

'Shey, I'm the one who has the excuse for drifting off. You said you see it now. What did you mean?' Uncle Freddy drew Shey back to the hospital room. The reassuring bleep of monitors. The hubbub from the activity that surrounded them.

'Age is whatever you think it is. You are as old as you think you are.'

'Well, yes, I think there is truth in that.'

'Except, it's not true. You know Muhammad Ali is supposed to have said that? A sentiment expressed by many people over the years.[4] And yes, retaining vitality is to some extent a state of mind. To a point.' Shey felt suddenly very emotional. Tears were close.

'Uncle, once again you teach me a profound life lesson. We must push at the boundaries, search for meaning and purpose, but, and this is probably the toughest lesson I've learned so far, we must work constantly to resist putting aspects of our lives on autopilot. We like to think each time we conquer a life challenge we check done and move on. The problem is that things change. Our work changes, the rules change, the circumstances change. But they are the tip of the iceberg. The submerged part changes too. Our relationships, our family, our support mechanism. They are hard to see. But the hardest of all is behind our own eyes. We are changing. We are ageing. Our bodies, minds. Yes, slowly but inevitably.

'Yes, this is why Muhammad Ali was wrong. The bigger challenge, the greater truism, is that it is much easier to point out how everyone else is changing than to accept your own journey through life phases. We live in a world that celebrates those who fight against the establishment. Who push the boundaries of conventions. However, ignoring how we need different things at 37 then we did at 23 or will at 75 makes about as much sense as believing AI will end the world. AI is a tool like so many others we have invented over the years. It's how we adapt to them that matters.'

Shey and Uncle Freddy looked at one another for what seemed like a long time.

'If you think I'm coming to live with your mother and father you've got another thing coming young man! Over my dead body!' Uncle Freddy smiled.

'Well, hopefully it won't come to that. Would it make a difference if I get them to embrace macOS?'[5]

₭⊳

'I love you all!' Shey paused to say one last goodbye to the gathered crowd of well-wishers. 'Don't be sad people. This is good. Change is good. It's taken me a while to understand that reinvention is not just a good thing. It's the only way to live a good life. We must look forward, not try to hold onto the past.'

'Be careful in the Big Apple. Make sure you call every week,' said mum.

'Look up the people I told you about,' said dad. 'They are great contacts and whatever you do next they can be good allies for you.'

'Give our love to Babs,' said Ellen. 'We plan to visit once the craziness of the next few weeks are behind us. Between getting the kids settled and working on my global kitchen venture. I know this is good for you Shey.

If nothing else, we will look forward to the vacation we have planned. Climbing Kilimanjaro will be awesome.'

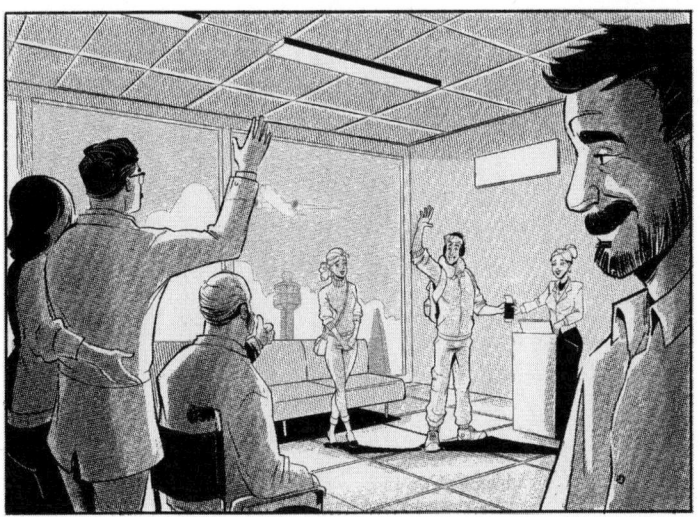

'Shey,' Uncle Freddy really looked so much better. 'I should have finished building the tunnel to escape in the next week. I'll look you up when I cross into Switzerland.' He was revelling in his prisoner of mum and dad persona. 'Honestly, one more attempt to feed me bone broth and I plan to invoke the Geneva Convention.'

'Mr Sinope, I am glad to have had this adventure with you.' Shey was surprised but happy Angelos had come to say farewell. 'Detective stories are so often tragedies. But sometimes to move forward the present must be violently disrupted. Then like the phoenix, amazing things can grow.'

With that Shey walked down the jetway. Yes, he thought, reinvention is good. But it also sucks. It's a shame we can't just keep the most important precious things in stasis. Although that would entail imprisoning people you love and stopping them from pursuing their own dreams. And that would be perverse. Ultimately, as a wise person once said… if you love them… you must set them free… and he was now free.

PART II
AVOIDING PROFESSIONAL OBSOLESCENCE

Chapter 15

Artificial Death of a Career – Introduction to Part II

Our Shey Sinope story is designed to provide you with an entertaining tale with some deeper messages. The focus of this book, at its core, is to discuss the subject of career reinvention. To look at how life can get in the way. How, particularly in your middle career years, you can end up vulnerable to falling victim to major business cycles or new technology adoption.

There are many business books dedicated to discussing how organizations do and don't succeed in navigating waves of disruption. They seek to pinpoint the secrets of reinvention at the business level. We have read our fair share of these, and they *are* essential reading. Whether you have to read them for an MBA or choose to read them to educate yourself on the distinctive attributes and traits that appear necessary for large scale organizations to successfully navigate change.

Good to Great, Only the Paranoid Survive, Leading Change say important things about how existing organizations adapt. On the other side of the equation *Exponential Organizations* and *The Innovator's Dilemma* provide insights on fast-moving entrepreneurial start-ups.[1,2,3,4,5] We've made the observation that some of these books, while containing indispensable knowledge, require a certain dedication and stamina. When you read Michael Porter's thoughts on competitive advantage, for example, few people we've met have described it as a 'fun' or 'engaging' read.[6] Essential, yes. Sort of like a dentist visit, or a colonoscopy. It's often easier to read the blink summaries. We find more often what resonates with people are the stories and the embedded wisdom in fascinating biographies from the likes of Walter Isaacson, or the compelling first-person narratives from entrepreneurs in *Shoe Dog*, *Grinding it Out* or indeed Michael Lewis' always insightful cautionary tales like *Liars Poker* and *The Big Short*.[7,8,9,10]

This book, consequently, seeks to distinguish itself by looking at reinvention from two very specific and unique perspectives. First, we are interested in helping you, the reader. How can we individually make the best choices? Help prepare for our own personal need for professional reinvention? Better navigate the conflicting, confusing, and complex emotions, urges, misinformation, misdirection, and only too human miscalculations, to win the battle within ourselves? In our experience, these are often far more important and essential than the external forces we really don't control. More importantly, where much is written about the economic winds that constantly toy with the international oceans of commerce, there is almost nothing written that helps us understand how to personally navigate these unpredictable seas.

The second distinction is that we seek to make these subjects accessible. Our view is that it is counterproductive to take a really important subject and cloak it in layers of complexity, analysis, and academic jargon. So, this book is designed to be an antidote to that. A book about career reinvention that is relevant, entertaining, and fun.

Part I of our book was designed specifically for those people, like us, who enjoy reading a story that entertains while prompting reflection. The story is, at a basic level, a cautionary tale about getting lost and distracted in your professional life. Of how the complexity of our wider lives can play a role in confusing us. Of how success doesn't guarantee continued success. And poses the following questions: 'Are you also vulnerable to suffering the same career breakdown that Shey suffers in our story?' and 'How do you figure out if you are losing your way, starting to sleepwalk professionally?' and finally, 'How can you avoid falling victim to career obsolescence?'

In Part II, we will supplement the pure storytelling piece with the behavioural science, executive coaching, and career planning explanations. We will also share some real-life career stories from some extraordinary people. In doing so, we will give those of you interested in delving more deeply into the substance some sustenance. Part I is designed for right-brain thinking and Part II left-brain thinking. This said, we promise to continue to keep the approach practical and straightforward.

Life phases present profound challenges

In our Introduction, we provided a commentary on how human beings have proven resilient as a species. We pointed to the long list of major inflection points in our history. Enough of us have adapted not only to survive but also to thrive. Few people would dispute that today's human civilization is a significant improvement in almost every way from those of the stone age, iron age, medieval, and industrial revolution. It does however leave the intriguing question: why do some of us fail to embrace these waves of change that have ultimately benefited our broader society?

Many people find it very hard to adapt. Indeed, some of us actively resist it. The question we are exploring in this book is why that happens. Why is it that some of us struggle to adapt when faced with overwhelming evidence that change is necessary, required, essential, beneficial? Do we lack the skills? Do we lack the information? What stops us?

In our view, the answer to these questions might be something surprising. In our experience, the people who struggle to adapt to change have fallen foul of a wilful blindness. A behavioural malady that has led them to believe they are either immune to wider changes taking place or they see no sense of urgency, no existential threat. Like people sleepwalking towards a cliff of irrelevance. How is this possible? How is it that otherwise rational people would walk, of their own volition, toward a sheer cliff that could kill their careers?

The answer? Well, it's a very natural and human instinct. Something deeply coded inside us. Something of an eternal challenge. As long as we humans have been capable of thought, we have had to make sense of the world around us. To know our place in it. The natural life phases we, as humans, experience make us interpret and answer that question in different ways. Most of the great religions in the world have attempted to categorize our life phases. Greeks, Jews, Hindus, medieval Europeans have all attempted to categorize the distinctive aspects of how we relate to childhood, adolescence, adulthood, parental, and old age.[11] We would also point to Gail Sheehy's celebrated book *Passages: Predictable Crises of Adult Life* built on the research by renown sociologists and psychologists Erik Erikson and Roger Gould.[12,13,14] A part of Gail's genius was her irresistible turn of phrase. She gifted us the memorable terms *Trying Twenties, Catch 30*, and *Deadline Decade*, along with the umbrella of midlife crisis.

The research and science reinforce what we intuitively know. As we grow and develop as human beings, we experience profound changes in our perspectives. Our lives become more complex, more diverse. We, quite naturally, re-evaluate what is important as we learn, experience new feelings, new emotions, and search for deeper meaning from life. We place greater importance on different facets of our lives. And it follows that we come to leave some things we previously thought important behind.

When we are children, we focus on our parents, our family, on going to school and being a good student. Our goals are to have fun, get good grades, and please our parents. When we are adolescents, we start to worry about what others think of us. We become more concerned with our role in a wider community. We are consumed by self-consciousness and wanting to be attractive to other people.

Then we enter professional life.

Professional life is a major step for us. From dependency to independence. We are fighting to become self-sufficient. This propels our early careers. We are fuelled by a desperation to prove we can 'adult'. In our experience, this transition is one of the four big inflection points in our professional lives. A gravitational force that consumes us for five to ten years as we try to establish a degree of separation and independence from parents.

What happens next? When you have proven you can find a space in the professional world and compete successfully. When you have your own home and can pay your bills, maybe even vacation somewhere nice. Well, lots of things follow, working through who you really are, what love means to you, what makes you happy. It's like you raise your head above the furore of winning at work and start to look for answers to deeper more sustaining aspects of life.

A consequence of this diversification, broadening of your horizons, is that your job becomes less central, less vital. Indeed, you start to relax. Start to be more comfortable that work is just work. It's a routine. It's a transaction. An enabler. A necessary evil.

You start to take work for granted. You explore other aspects of life. You reconnect, reframe, and recontract with family. In some ways you see this re-engagement with family and friends as far more important than professional life. You become aware, suddenly, that some important people won't be around forever. Friends start to pose new questions about whether your friendship means something beyond an occasional night out and sharing jokes. You start to think about children, the wider world, suffering, injustice. Shouldn't you dedicate some of your time to help make the place better?

And then, out of the blue, one rainy Tuesday morning, your boss calls you into her office and says: 'I'm really sorry about this… please understand… it is *NOT PERSONAL… IT IS JUST BUSINESS…*'

Artificial Death of a Career

The consequence of this changing perspective and re-evaluation of what is most critical in our lives is that we quite naturally start to lose the hunger and fear that drives our early career motivations. As we segue into our middle careers, there is a danger of complacency. This is the basis for our story *Artificial Death of a Career*.

The starting point for the story is how our lives become very confusing and complicated. Success in no way insulates or makes us immune to complacency. In some ways, it makes it even more tempting. It's a misnomer to believe that greater access to power, money, resources will mean that we avoid losing our way.

In our story, we paint the picture of Shey in his late 30s sleepwalking toward obsolescence. We loved the idea of using AI as part of the central storyline. So many articles and so much commentary has been focused on a fear of AI. How it will erode one of the last bastions of human capability... the knowledge worker. In our story, however, we take the starting position for many of the most popularized myths about AI and try to turn it around. So, the set-up is presenting El Gin as a very sophisticated machine that appears to have gone rogue... lost its marbles!

However, then we try to turn it around to point out that ultimately, Shey is the chief architect of his own demise. Along the way, we toy with the idea of AI being some malevolent super intelligence, when the reality, at least today, is something else. The inconvenient truth about AI is that it isn't what people think it is.

We suspect many of you will have figured out the Greek, Elgin Marbles, thread that runs throughout the story. In British English, there is this phrase 'losing one's marbles'. We have stretched this for our story to be an interpretation of how Shey has lost his way professionally but also used it for the storytelling value. Hopefully, all of our Greek friends will forgive us. After all, it was a gift (horse) we couldn't refuse.

We punctuated the story with the growing sophistication story for El Gin. This was designed to suggest a path to self-awareness that is easily misconstrued. The thread about giraffes is based in truth.[15] As is the basis for explaining how 'narrow' AI does not lead magically to 'general' AI... no matter how many labradors you wire together.[16] However, we were also keen to balance our sense that AI was being labelled 'a witch' with the very reasonable observation that there could well be unintended consequences of this new technology. Of course, how better to illustrate that than to have Shey, a vocal defender of AI, end up falling victim to it!

The backdrop to our entire story is the suggestion that business isn't personal. This was our way of weaving a thread throughout Shey's journey that points to some powerful gravitational forces. Business is not a charity. It is not a welfare programme, and it is not always 'nice'. Perhaps this is obvious. However, you may be surprised by the number of people who talk about how their jobs are unfair, how they believe they are entitled to something different, or how their employer is only interested in profits. Now, we are not suggesting that business leaders, owners, and big companies shouldn't be responsible. Just abiding by a law is not sufficient justification for some corporate action (or inaction). There are moral and ethical questions that must be considered. This said, capitalism works fundamentally on a profit motive. Sometimes we think there are some strange beliefs and distortions in what business is all about. We have chosen to add that piece to our story.

Perhaps, as you read the story, you couldn't help but to think ahead. Start to speculate on what will happen. The idea of establishing *Artificial Death of a Career* on a murder/mystery/thriller format was a very deliberate choice. When we are told something is a mystery, we are prepared to look for clues. To play along with the authors' game. What happened exactly? Who did it? Who are the suspects? What pieces of the story are real clues versus red herrings? Attempts at misdirection.

This is important for our wider purpose. We want to pose the question, why are we less vigilant in our real lives. Why do we allow ourselves to stop looking for clues... to stop speculating on whodunnit and why? When Shey is fired as CEO of FEEL VR, he is stunned, shocked, angry... aggrieved. In a word, he is blindsided.

And this is the essential point.

We have rarely met someone who has been negatively impacted by a major business cycle, who didn't express shock, surprise, along with indignation, anger, a deep sense of having been wronged. In the story, we manifest these things through Shey's sense of having been assassinated. And all the corresponding projection that *someone else* must be to blame.

When we find ourselves victim of corporate downsizing, restructuring, or other bad work outcomes, we almost always look to blame someone else. 'It wasn't fair,' we complain. Some parts of our economy try to fight against modernization in the form of protectionism, closed shops, industrial action. 'Progress,' they shout, 'is fine... so long as it happens somewhere else!' We take no specific issue with workers' rights, organized labour, and the valid fights to balance corporate greed with a more balanced, fairer economic equation. But... our point is about being honest and clear-eyed in owning your own role and place in these natural, eternal, economic renewal cycles.

In *Artificial Death of a Career*, we follow Shey as he searches for who is to blame. He peels back the layers of suspects until, ultimately, he is left face to face with himself. Here, we conjure the picture of him walking down the rows of servers in the BUZBY warehouse, looking at his giraffe costume reflection. Who is to blame for Shey's predicament? Shey of course. He is the architect of his own demise. He has conspired to build his own replacement. And he has forgotten the natural order of things. Time marches on, technology changes, capabilities improve, objectives shift. Everything is in motion. Albeit sometimes you can't quite see it day-by-day, minute-by-minute.

On a professional level Shey stood still while all those around him changed. Where once he had a clear set of professional objectives, he had allowed them to languish, to crumble, to evaporate. The deeper meaning we intended in the telling of *Artificial Death of a Career* is that setting important career goals for ourselves, finding a sense of direction and purpose, is vitally important. It's one of the things we must come to terms with through our early careers. Transitioning from naïve attempts to 'win' at work to find something more fulfilling. A purpose, a cause, an answer to the questions: 'Why am I doing this?' and 'What's this all for?'

The trouble is, we forget that answers to those questions have a shelf life. In a narrow sense, all goals have a time frame attached to them. When we think of KPIs, metrics, projects, plans, they all have a deadline. In Shey's case, he had painfully figured out his answers to the questions in his late 20s. He didn't want to be a corporate soldier. He wanted to work on something he believed in. He founded his FEEL VR company on the back of some profound soul searching and after facing fears of personal inadequacy. What emerged from that battle to understand himself was a new path, a new set of goals, a deeper conviction about what his professional life should look like.

Seven years later, some of those things had changed. The initial need to prove he could make it on his own had been accomplished. Breaking free from a corporate rat race, also accomplished. Proving that FEEL VR as a product was viable... also checked. Exploring who he was as a person, separate from how society might compartmentalize him... checked. The discovery process that was a part of his late 20s battle to understand and separate his own aspirations from the cumulated expectation of family, friends, society... checked.

The trouble is, Shey had not revisited these questions in any meaningful way. Having addressed the questions once, his implicit assumption was he was now free of them. That the conviction, purpose, and epiphany he experienced at that time would last forever.

Artificial Death of a Career tells the story of the consequences.

Setting out Part II

In this next section of our book, we plan to delve into the big themes. We will explore them with a view to provide you with a better understanding of Shey's story, what happened, why, and most importantly, how you might choose a different path.

Our first theme is the problem of **Drift**. For the vast majority of us, this challenge occurs once we have established ourselves in our professional lives. Generally, after the first seven to ten years in our careers, we have demonstrated we can compete; we can master most aspects of our jobs. At the same time, our lives become more complex. We are faced with two big reasons to put aspects of our work on autopilot. First, the work we are doing is less challenging, and we feel we have less to prove. Second, our wider life creates new sources of crises, experiences, and decisions that scream for our attention. Our first chapter will look at **Drift**, explain how and why it occurs, and how you create support mechanisms to help guard against its worst consequences.

Next, we will look at **Reinvention**. Throughout our careers, we will face the need to reinvent ourselves. Try as we might to avoid this, to find a quiet niche somewhere in the world that may be protected from the ravages and consequences of progress, we will eventually recognize change is inevitable. The only question is whether we anticipate and get ahead of it or become collateral damage. In this chapter, we will look at why change is inevitable, what we know about how to do it well, and what you can do to improve your approach.

One facet of *Artificial Death of a Career* was the '*it's not personal... just business.*' The lines between business, community, society, justice, fairness have in some cases become blurred. In particular, there are many occasions where we observe individuals have created a false sense of expectation in what may be included in their employer–employee contract. This is not entirely their fault as there are conflicting messages from some company leadership and even owners. The third chapter in Part II is dedicated to trying to encourage a healthy perspective on the realities of the business and professional world.

Finally, we have included a chapter on **Surfing the Complexity of Adult Life**. Our book is about professional life and building your ability to benefit from reinvention. However, a key part of our professional success is being able to keep a healthy balance in our personal lives. Our depiction of Shey trying to juggle the relentless shock waves in romantic, family, and friend circles is worthy of greater examination.

Jaron Soh
Co-founder & CEO of VODA

When asked to summarize his career, Jaron takes a reflective pause before sharing his journey. At the age of 31, he has navigated a diverse range of professional experience – but his story is less about accolades and more about finding authenticity in his work and life.

Navigating identity and expectations

Jaron grew up in Singapore, a society with rigid views on both success and identity. As a gay man, he often felt at odds with these expectations. 'I spent much of my early years feeling a need to prove myself,' he reflects. 'I carried a lot of shame regarding my sexuality, and the way I felt that I could compensate for this supposed deficiency is to excel in areas like academics and work.'

These feelings shaped Jaron's early years. He was top of his class in his high school and then graduated from LSE with First Class Honours. At university, he led two societies concurrently while running his first start-up, funded by a grant he won from the university pitch competition. A year after college, Jaron launched a venture-backed technology company, leading tech as Chief Product Officer for a fast-growing start-up.

From the outside, he appeared successful, holding a coveted role as a start-up founder, earning recognition for his work. But inside, he struggled to reconcile his accomplishments with a deeper desire for meaning and authenticity.

He describes the inner conflict he was trying to manage. 'Everyone wants to belong; to believe they have made people proud. For a long time, I was driven by a sense that I was somehow inadequate, and so I had to find ways to compensate by working harder, achieving more, faster.'

Jaron says it took him a long time to unpick these conflicting emotions and understand what was behind his behaviours. 'I think we are all capable of doing great things. But we are also capable of high levels of self-deception and avoidance.'

Finding clarity in a moment of crisis

During the social isolation of the pandemic, while undergoing therapy, Jaron noticed a common struggle among his LGBTQIA+ friends: a lack of accessible, affirming mental health support.

This struck a chord with his own experiences and sparked an idea. 'I realized that I had the skills and the opportunity to create something meaningful, not just for others but also for myself.'

This clarity led him to leave his secure job and take a bold step toward building VODA, the LGBTQIA+ mental health app. The transition wasn't easy – it required him to confront his own fears and societal expectations.

He also needed to have difficult conversations with loved ones. 'To be the founder and CEO of a LGBTQIA+ mental health company meant I also needed to come out to my family.'

Building something that matters

Three years after its founding, VODA has grown into a platform that serves tens of thousands of LGBTQIA+ individuals globally. The app offers guided therapy programmes tailored to the unique challenges faced by the community, such as navigating gay shame, coming out, and gender dysphoria. Their work has won multiple awards and was named 'Rising Star' in the UK National Start-up Awards across thousands of companies.

'What makes VODA special is that it centres the LGBTQIA+ experience in mental health,' Jaron explains. 'It's not just about filling a gap – it's about creating a space where people feel seen and supported.'

He reflects on how VODA has changed his own life: 'The thing is, in many ways, VODA has also saved me. Without wanting to be too dramatic, what I mean is that without VODA, I might still be drifting through professional life pretending to be someone I really wasn't. It not only allowed me to do something meaningful, but it also gave me the opportunity to live my authentic life. I confronted necessary but difficult conversations with family. Whatever happens next, I will be grateful for where that has led.'

Career tip

Jaron's advice to young professionals is simple: take the time to reflect. 'Each year, ask yourself whether your work aligns with who you are and what you care about. Be careful you don't drift down a path not aligned with your values.

'Finding purpose isn't about having all the answers – it's about being willing to ask the right questions and take the first step toward change.'

By committing fully to something he cares deeply about, Jaron has found that work can become more than a career – it can be a way of living authentically and meaningfully. And for him, that's a journey worth taking.

Chapter 16

Professional Drift

'Give me the opportunity and I promise you one thing... no one will ever work harder for you than me.' 'I need this job. Getting this job is the single most important thing in my life.' 'I'll do anything for this promotion, my entire future, everything that matters to me is dependent on achieving this next step!'

Sound familiar? We talk with lots of people setting out in professional life. There is often a singular focus, a complete fixation on acquiring their first job, first promotion, first bonus. At its worst, it can be an obsession, a temptation to collapse their lives into this one goal. We too remember our own experiences early in our careers. We understand how it feels. There is sense of embarking on something where the odds are stacked against you. A David and Goliath challenge. You are the underdog, attempting to compete against seasoned pros in an alien corporate game of gladiators.

When we start out on our careers, we must overcome many obstacles. There is the *Work Experience Deficit Paradox*, for example.[1] The strange dynamic where most jobs require prior work experience... but if you don't have any... how do you get some? The job-hunting system, the corporate hiring process, and then discovering how the system of promotions and pay raises work is all incredibly confusing and intimidating.

At the same time, most of us are at stages of our lives where transitioning from dependants of our parents to stand instead on our own two feet is paramount. Yes, we have friends, relatives, and interests beyond work. However, they are often demoted in our priorities. A lot of this is quite natural and unconscious, but the result is we will find ourselves placing work-related matters ahead of family and friend commitments. Simply put, we make a calculation that finding a good job, establishing ourselves in the professional world, facilitates some critical first order essentials; housing, travel, clothes, the ability to make independent decisions about what, where, and how we go about living our lives.

It's a thankless job but someone has to do it

'Hey, I do what I'm told. I'm only here for the pay cheque.' 'Yeah, I really don't care whether it makes sense. I just do what they tell me to.' 'I'm checked out at work. There are more important things in life.' 'I feel like a robot at work.' 'I've earned the right to slow down a bit. I let the bright young things do the running around and volunteering for new stuff.'

Also sound familiar? How often have you heard someone you know talk disparagingly about their jobs? Have you too made similar comments, entertained comparable thoughts? Some people do go through life with a very transactional, contractual, disconnected relationship with work. Generally, however, we all seem to transition from desperate attempts to compete at work, to more cynical and reluctant job hostages.

So, what changes? What happens to those of us who transition from naïve Duracell bunnies, intent on outworking and outperforming to become corporate zombies?

Life happens.

Work is a priority until it's not

We have framed the contrasting outlooks on the role work plays in our lives along a temporal spectrum. There are, of course, some people who never develop more than a transactional relationship with work. The so-called 'work to live' demographic. There are a few people who try hard to compartmentalize work by holding it at an emotional distance. There are even some who reject traditional capitalist professions, preferring to dedicate themselves to more altruistic and spiritual causes.

Regardless, we make the point that whatever life pursuit you may choose, how you look at it will change with time. The idealism and boundless energy of youth slowly subsides into a more measured equilibrium of middle and old age. Along the way, other interests, ideas, priorities make themselves known to us. The world forces new information, concepts, technologies, experiences, and people into our lives. In the process, with every small, incremental event, our perspective is nudged, ever so slightly. Even if we could isolate ourselves from the world, go live in a cave somewhere in the middle of an uninhabited desert, our inner human time clock would change our perspective. There is a profound difference in how we think about life and what's ahead when we are 20, 30, 40, or 60.

The science behind professional drift

There are two primary strands of research that help inform what causes professional drift. The first has been popularized recently in the form of *Boreout* and *Quiet Quitting*.[2,3] While the labels suggest something recent, they are both built on long established neuroscience.

Both *Boreout* and *Quiet Quitting* describe finding yourself in situations where you have no emotional attachment to your work. In fact, they suggest a rather dystopian experience of having your energy zapped by layers of poor management, organizational confusion, and job tasks that are boring, tedious, and repetitive. They are different dimensions of the same dynamic. The (unintended) consequences of companies who have created poor work environments. In both cases, the suggestion is that the problem is the offending companies' systems, processes, quality of leadership, and for want of a better word, culture.

From an individual standpoint, the reason we feel disengaged is explained through neuroscience. In her fascinating book *Wired to Resist: The Brain Science of Why Change Fails*, Britt Andreatta points out how the *basal ganglia* function in our brains takes repetitive tasks and helps us convert them into unconscious actions.[4] Sort of like a behavioural autopilot. From learning to ride a bike, through working on an assembly line, to attending a long tedious meeting, our brains ingeniously create background programmes that they unconsciously trigger for us. The capability helps us spend more time on more important things. The problem, of course, is that if most of your job involves these kinds of repetitive tasks, well, you end up twiddling your thumbs and waiting for the excuse to log off for the day.

Many of us intuitively accept that at least some aspects of our work are likely to be boring. We make some calculation about whether, on balance, 51% of the work we do engages us enough to put up with the rest. Should the equation go the wrong way, when we think rationally, we start to look at making a change in our careers. We search for something better and plot a course accordingly. Strangely, however, some of us persevere. Why would rational people choose to continue in jobs that are completely unfulfilling, boring, repetitive, and soul crushing?

The *habenula* function in our brains may be the reason. The habenula is the part of our brain that controls the releases of dopamine and serotonin. The feel-good chemicals that we hear so much about. However, it also works to avoid punishment. Dr Okihide Hikosaka of the National Institutes of Health Laboratory of Sensorimotor Research has found that it actively suppresses our motivation to take on any new tasks where we fear we might fail.[5] If we frame work as a necessary evil, as something that requires sacrifice and suffering, it is quite natural for us to avoid change for fear it will only lead to more suffering. Or, indeed, we even come to believe that work and suffering are synonymous.

We understand how our brains naturally create processes that could lead us to become distracted at work. To put aspects, perhaps the majority, of our jobs on autopilot. This helps explain one reason why, as time goes by, there is a greater danger of us spending less time thinking about work, our jobs, our careers. However, there is also how we change our perspectives on life as we grow older. Earlier, we pointed to how our lives become more complex, diverse, and dispersed as we grow older. We shared some of the attempts from ancient Greek philosophers, through religious teachings, to modern psychologists to point out the distinctive perspective shifts we make as we grow older.

Few of us would dispute that there are profound differences between how we view the world in our childhood versus adulthood, and then old age. Life-phase research helps us understand how our journey through life confronts us with distinctive challenges. As we grow older, we navigate independence from parents, become parents ourselves, come to terms with our own mortality, deal with our parents ageing, and everything in between.

Gail Sheehy helps us underline this dynamic. She conjured the phrases *Trying 20s*, *Catch 30s*, and *Forlorn 40s*, to illustrate how our perspectives change as we grow older.[6] In our 20s, we search for our own deeper identity, trying to separate ourselves from parental and societal expectations. In our 30s, we find ourselves fighting to balance wider commitments with our professional goals. In simple terms, we broaden our consciousness which helps us grow as human beings, but that distracts our attention from professional goals. Indeed, they start to make us question our priorities, where we spend our time, and whether work is as central as we thought it was.

And then there are the *Forlorn 40s*... coming to terms with our own mortality, the fast-evaporating time to do all the things we wanted to do. Whether we call this midlife crisis, or as many researchers now believe, the vertex low point of our personal optimism, it is a fraught period for us to navigate.[7] We start out in our childhood filled with great hopes and dreams. By our late 30s and 40s, we are generally faced with different realities. We must come to terms with the dissonance. The good news... from 40 to 70, we start to rediscover some of the lost optimism.

The psychologist Donald Super in the 1950s was the first to take our evolution through life phases and translate them into how they may impact our careers.[8] He theorized we experience five stages from launch to decline, focusing on how we progress from apprentices to masters of our chosen professions. While the work of Super, Erikson (who we mentioned earlier), and Sheehy provide valuable insights, we think individually they miss an important point. As we move through our careers, we get distracted by aspects of our natural development and growth as human beings. We start to experience limits to our emotional capacity.

When we are seeking our first job, our lives tend to be simpler, more streamlined, more focused. While there are always exceptions, we may start our first job between the ages of 18 and 24 and attempt to stand on our own two feet. Our friends and families will be in attendance, supporting, perhaps even subsidizing us. In our mid-30s, some aspects are now routine, no longer novel.

We have proven we can survive, have become more confident, and even complacent about work. Plus, and this is the key point, we start to build families of our own, and emotionally move further away from our paternal cradles. The natural circle of things. We create space for ourselves to explore other facets of life: meaning, happiness, individual identity, and causes to champion.

The context for life is very different in our 30s versus late teens and early 20s. And that context can be distracting. It can make you re-evaluate what is important to you. Re-prioritize where you spend your time. Effect how you think about work. For example, at 24 you work long hours because you want to prove something to yourself and others. At 37, you don't feel that same urgency. In fact, you may feel you have earned the right to take the foot of the pedal. Why shouldn't you leave work early? Why shouldn't you take care of some personal things during work hours? Why should you try as hard, care as much? There are other things that matter more.

Shey's professional drift in *Artificial Death of a Career*

In our story, we illustrate these points. We introduce Shey as a successful, sought after, entrepreneur. We intended to depict Shey in the throes of dealing with the minutia of business. Meetings, conferences, human resource matters. We have the story set on the outskirts of the post-COVID return to the office controversary.

We deliberately obfuscated the core business goals and original purpose of FEEL VR. However, if we contrast where this story begins with what originally inspired Shey to launch FEEL VR, he has lost focus. For those of you who haven't yet read *A Groundhog Career* where FEEL VR was introduced, Shey was intent on fixing a problem.[9] He had a clear sense of purpose. An overarching cause. What Keiran Setiya, the MIT philosophy professor, calls *atelic* rather than *telic* goals, distinguishing between tasks that have a finality versus those that are pursuits without an obvious end.[10] Shey invented his FEEL VR headset with a view to trying to increase the world's empathy. He made the observation that social media and technology had left the world with an empathy deficit. Shey believed he could do something about that. He could help the world become a more caring, kinder, better place.

Fast forward seven years from the launch of FEEL VR and Shey is now dealing with return to the office policies, not because they are critical to the success of the business, but because he is lonely. He is no longer focused on the outcomes, the purpose of his invention. Instead, he is consumed by the tactical and administrative. His focus has changed, become more short term, more transactional… more *telic*.

We amplify this drift by the El Gin invention. El Gin, the clever AI system that runs much of Shey's business. And this is the crux of how Shey has lost his way, albeit unconsciously. He has incrementally delegated, automated, transferred so many aspects of his business that he has lost sight of the bigger picture. Ironically, perhaps, the idea of an integrated technology platform, pulling together and aggregating data across a business is often cited as a means to improve business decision making. We point out that it also creates a reliance, a crutch, a laziness. If the software can make these decisions for us, well, we will just trust it to do so and busy ourselves with other things. In the process we lose sight of critical information, context, and insights. We become less connected, more marginalized, more superfluous.

Indeed, not only has Shey lost sight of his original purpose for FEEL VR, but he has also become distracted by venture capital valuations, and the political power games that go along with corporate governance systems. This fuels his mistrust and feeling of indignation when Jian Xu shares the unexpected news that he is being replaced. Shey was looking in the wrong direction. Rather than stick to his knitting, remaining focused on his original purpose, staying close to his core convictions about what FEEL VR was all about, he was instead operating in a very blinkered, almost scattergun way. The classic *forest for the trees* metaphor, or more to the point, successful entrepreneur invents amazing product but then gets lost in the execution phase… struggling to understand how CEO and founder are distinct and different skills.

Of course, the wider context complicates and distracts. On a professional level, Shey is celebrated for his invention. This creates a sense of invulnerability. Provides ammunition to fuel an ego. Being invited to conferences and reading articles that celebrate your genius and farsightedness are not great ingredients to keep you grounded.

And this is where the drift in Shey's wider life has also contributed to his distraction. He is navigating some momentous life events. His romantic partner is moving to New York... unexpectedly. His best friend is literally under fire in Palestine. And his beloved Uncle is in intensive care. We all are destined to experience similar although we hope less dramatic personal challenges. We wanted to underline how Shey is experiencing some profound shifts in his life. Of how his personal universe is reordering itself, the tectonic plates in constant motion. Shey, however, hasn't been paying attention. He continues to go about his routine as if nothing has changed. He has been sleepwalking. Much of his life on autopilot. We underline this by presenting the big personal events as great surprises that are greeted with shock, disbelief, denial. Our intention is to leave the lingering question, could, and indeed should, Shey have recognized the signposts along the way?

We weave these themes into our story to point to how such events make you (1) think about how we can find ourselves conflicted about the role that work plays in our wider lives, and (2) be the cause of a significant distraction, one that steadily grows through our late 20s, 30s and 40s. When you once laid awake in bed thinking of some work problem, that space is superseded by other, more important worries. The reason there is no Olympic medal for worrying is that there would be 8 billion winners. We are champions at finding things to worry, fret, and obsess about. And, of course, the other dimension is that our personal support network, the one that would normally help us navigate through professional crises, well, they are distracted dealing with their own troubles.

The consequences of professional drift

Like the saying goes, if you are looking for the wrong things, you will eventually find them. Professional drift, at its core, is allowing yourself to lose focus, interest, enthusiasm, energy to look at your career, your work, and continually challenge yourself to reach further, strive for something new, interesting, engaging. It's like crossing a busy street. Who is to blame if you aren't carefully paying attention before you step off the curb? If you look only left when the traffic is coming from the right? To arrogantly assume the traffic will stop for you because you have earned the right to cross the street whenever and however you wish.

In *Artificial Death of a Career*, we point to the board's decision to replace Shey as CEO. This is one of the consequences of professional drift. Redundancy, obsolescence. However, it isn't the only consequence. Our research points to the following:

1. **Passivity over Proactivity**: There is a correlation between professional drift and a deepening sense of disillusionment. A self-fulfilling prophecy that creates a vicious circle where people who lose interest, find themselves operating more and more on autopilot. In turn, their employers, bosses, organizations no longer seek them out for interesting new work assignments. They are overlooked for promotions. The wheel turns and disillusionment and disengagement increases…

2. **Protectionist over Pioneer**: Drift leads to us losing interest in looking forward professionally.

When we stop paying attention to new trends, technology, and opportunities, we become prisoners of backward thinking. We become interested and vested in trying to protect the status quo. This is the Luddite perspective.[11] Choosing to place a great importance on protecting your existing position, status, living. Fighting a rearguard battle to protect what you have.

3. **Victimhood over Opportunist**: When our attention drifts away from actively engaging in our careers, in what we are doing now and what might be ahead for us, we lose sight of the flow of traffic, of the direction of the winds. This leads to us being 'surprised' by entirely predictable events.

If we had a pound for every story we heard about people being blindsided by a major corporate redundancy programme, a bankruptcy, a major economic cycle, a change in regulatory regime, or the introduction of AI, well… we would be several hundred pounds richer. For example, we learned recently of someone who was called on a Monday morning at 7am.

'I know you are at the airport on your way to New York. I need you to change flights. Come to Sunnyvale, California, instead.' Their boss told them. The company had just been acquired and the person was being asked to meet at the new company's headquarters.

The person's response is what fascinates us, 'Oh my gosh… what's happened?'

It is possible that a company can be unexpectedly acquired. It is also possible that a bankruptcy or some other *force majeure* could detrimentally affect your job, work, career. But... this was a technology company who had been actively and publicly the subject of acquisition discussions for six months. Cases like this make us genuinely worried and concerned when people seem to ignore the obvious signals, breadcrumbs, and bullhorns blaring: BEWARE! BEWARE! IMMINENT EXTINCTION EVENT!

Professional drift leads to a wilful blindness. It makes you much more vulnerable to career shocks and crises. Choose your analogy, driving only looking in the mirror, sleepwalking toward a thousand-foot cliff, a passenger on a small rudderless boat being tossed by an angry ocean.

An antidote to professional drift

We hope we have provided you with a compelling argument for how we become distracted in our 30s and 40s. Of how 'life' happens to us. We can point to countless examples of people we have worked with who have apparently woken up one day to an unwelcome realization; they are facing a crisis. From being the victim of a significant corporate downsizing, to losing sleep for worry of being replaced by AI, there are too many examples of people who have become detached, asleep at the wheel when it comes to their careers. Feeling powerless, an unwitting victim of overwhelming forces is, to some extent, a personal choice. One where we lose interest, energy, enthusiasm to proactively, aggressively, and assertively take ownership of our own futures.

The good news is that you can change this if you want to. And here is something that might shock you, it's not incredibly difficult to turn this around. To flip the switch from being distracted, complacent, and instead force yourself to look forward, plan for what is ahead professionally. Make sure you stay relevant by remembering the benefits of **CAFFEINE**. We are fond of mnemonic devices, and we think this one works well in the context of waking up but also our general fixation with coffee:

C = Cues. There are natural events in our life that occur every year. For example, our work anniversaries, the end of the calendar year, our birthdays. These are natural events that can help us take time to find the space to drop out from the day-to-day tyranny of work and find the space to ask yourself some important questions: What is happening in your industry? What is happening with your organization? Where will both be in five to ten years? What implications does that have for you?

A = Argument. Debating the state of your job, profession and industry with a group of work colleagues, a mentor, a college professor can be a rewarding and fun experience. We all like to try to predict the future. Challenge yourself to find a mechanism at least once a year to exchange predictions with like-minded individuals. Like a career fantasy football league.

F = Fun. Things like fantasy career leagues also fit into the fun category. However, we would also cite things like learning new skills, discovering something new about your company, your industry, and the technology that is on the horizon. We have set monthly challenges for people in our teams to teach themselves something new and then share it.

F = Forecast. Making an annual forecast of where you plan to be in one, three, five, and ten years is at the core of staying relevant. Take an annual inventory and set yourself new goals every year.

E = Example. If we can imagine it, we can do it. This is very true in our experience. Seek out individuals in your profession who are energetic about their careers, your profession, and perhaps life more generally. Ask them to mentor you or just find ways to spend time with them regularly. We all need some upbeat energy in our lives; this is just as important at work as it is at home.

I = Incentive. If you need it, give yourself a reward for completing annual inventories and reviews of where you are in your career. It can be powerful to link your reviews to some personal ambition, like climbing Machu Picchu, Kilimanjaro, or running a marathon!

N = Nudges. Sending yourself reminders, making calendar entries, and asking someone to make sure you fulfil them can be powerful life hacks. There are even some great new digital tools that help create commitments for us, like *StickK* and *Beeminder*.[12,13] We suggest you think about experimenting with them.

E = Educate. One of our favourite examples is recommending people consider teaching. It's a great way to stay relevant in your field and in the process, surround yourself with people who are typically starting out in their careers. This has the double benefit of forcing you to read up on what's new and changing in your profession but also surrounding yourself with that infectious naïve enthusiasm.

Did you know that, according to some behavioural economists who study how people relate to changing behaviours, there are just two types of people: 'sophisticates' and 'naifs'.[14] The theory is that most of us acknowledge we have behavioural obstacles, tendencies, and flaws that result in us doing irrational things. Where the 'naifs' go wrong is that they are overly optimistic about their ability to change through sheer willpower or believe that the need for change can be delayed, deferred. Sadly, these are the people who tend to wake up one day to the news that they have been blindsided by some 'unexpected' news.

The 'sophisticates' approach things differently. They act to help ensure they confront their counterproductive tendencies. Having read this far, we think you should feel like you have already crossed a line from 'naif' and are well on your way to 'sophisticate'.

Chapter reflection exercises

The big challenge with professional drift is being unconscious of how our surrounding context erodes our relevance. The **CAFFEINE** mnemonic provides some prompts to counter the root causes of professional drift. However, to further sharpen and increase your vigilance, to make you a true sophisticate, we offer the following reflection exercises:

1. **Professional Prediction Fantasy League**
   - Agree with two or three work colleagues, mentors, or college professors to compare your annual predictions for how your profession will be impacted over three, five, ten years.

Include the following in your prediction:

- The mega-trends like generational demographics and attitudes, technology, access to knowledge, growing and ageing population, advances in medical care, political movements, regulation/legislation, and science.[15]
- The relative 'health' of your organization to survive and flourish given the above.
- Your personal resilience and confidence in remaining relevant and in demand given the above.

Our goal with this exercise is combining aspects of the Argument, Fun, Forecast, and Example components we discussed earlier. When we spend time, even if just annually, undertaking a top-down analysis of macro trends and draw preliminary conclusions about what they may mean to us, we awaken to risks and opportunities. We renew our enthusiasm for seeing our careers as a puzzle, a conundrum, a jigsaw. We are amazed at how good most people are at drawing value from this exercise.

Outcome: Write down your predictions and email them to yourself. Make a calendar entry six or 12 months out. Remind yourself to refresh the exercise. Always end each exercise with your two or three actions. How can you improve your own personal position in whatever prediction you make? How can you ensure that you remain awake and able to take advantage of whatever happens next in your career?

2. **Personal Universe Map**
    - Draw two lines in the shape of a classic X and Y graph.
    - Label the X axis 'proximity'.
    - Label the Y axis 'importance'.
    - Place the initials of your closest friends, confidantes, family, mentors, and other role models on the chart based on how they feel to you *today*.

It's easy to lose sight of how our personal universes are changing. One way to remind ourselves of small but important changes is to make a map and update it every year. We have undertaken this exercise both personally and with people we work with. If you do it annually and compare the results you will be astounded about how it shows. The extraordinary changes that take place each year in how some people move in and out of our personal orbits There are no wrong or right answers to this exercise, but the important point is to look at how things have changed and ask yourself what that means in the context of where you are spending your time, what you think is important, and whether things that were once true remain so.

The goal with both reflection exercises is to find ways to bring the unconscious into view. To make your radar much more accurate when it comes to highlighting the important changes that are taking place around you. When you have found a professional direction, it is too easy, too seductive, to put it on autopilot. This is a recipe to be blindsided by some calamitous but entirely predictable and preventable crisis.

Chapter blink

- We become more susceptible to *professional drift* in our middle careers.

- As we master our jobs, we put the more repetitive tasks on *autopilot*.

- As we do, we become more vulnerable to growing work disillusionment (*Boreout* and *Quiet Quitting*).

- Research in neurology helps explain these are natural and understandable behavioural responses.

- As we age, we experience profound changes in our outlook and perspective on life.

- Our *Trying 20s*, *Catch 30s*, and *Forlorn 40s* create very different contexts for the role that work plays in our lives.

- The consequence is we may *sleepwalk* toward professional *obsolescence*.

- However, many risks of redundancy, severance, professional declines are entirely predictable and avoidable.

- The antidote to professional drift is planning your career with *CAFFEINE*!

In three phrases

1. **Be Awake to Risk of Drift** – find ways to stay awake at the wheel.

2. **Life Happens to Us All** – recognize that we need to adapt our career approach for changing life circumstances.

3. **Sophisticates are Darwin's Darlings** – concrete plans beat leaps of faith.

Anna Joseph
Managing Partner at J&A Mentoring Partners

Anna's career is perhaps defined by being both extraordinary and unconventional.

Extraordinary in the sense that she has demonstrated virtuoso discipline, commitment, and performance in everything she has done. Unconventional because she started life apparently destined to be one of the world's great violinists, then found herself working for the renown McKinsey, before spending time helping UK FTSE 100 companies sharpen their marketing strategies and finally launching her own executive mentorship business.

'All of my childhood memories seem to involve music. All the pictures seem to involve me holding a violin,' she jokes. 'I started music lessons aged three, got my first violin at four, and performed publicly from age ten.' During her teenage years she climbed to the heady heights of performing as a soloist with orchestras like the LSO, live on BBC Radio 3, and completing a scholarship at the prestigious Julliard School in New York.

Anna is very modest about her long list of extraordinary career highlights. When it comes to explaining the apparent sharp twists and turns it has taken, she is disarmingly forthright. 'For a long time, I followed a path that was mapped out for me. I was immersed in a context that swept me along. I didn't really question it. Everyone around me assured me I was destined to be a violinist and so that's what I did.'

Everyone seems to think this is my destiny... except me

At age 23, arguably at the peak of musical success, Anna quit.

'It took me a year, almost totally in private, to consider whether I truly would walk away from the only deep engagement and identity I'd had to date. Meantime, my agent was booking concerts into the future, which felt like additional pressure of course.'

Anna recalls how stressed and conflicted she felt. There were people in her life that felt passionately she should continue in the music business and were not backward about coming forward. 'The most frightening thing was confronting all those who I felt I was letting down. Weirdly, at the same time, I don't remember being that worried about developing a plan B. While effectively I was jumping out of the airplane in mid-flight (without a parachute!), what I would do afterwards didn't seem to faze me as much as it could have done.'

Looking back now, with the wisdom of hindsight, and having found great success in the corporate and entrepreneurial worlds, Anna believes she was ultimately attempting to break free from the invisible external forces that had controlled, limited, defined, and constrained her.

'I wasn't happy. I had a vague sense of what might make me happy in terms of far greater involvement and close interaction with other people. But the critical thing was that I knew I would never find it unless I struck out on my own. Took the proverbial leap.'

A random walk to fulfilment

Anna describes her 20s and 30s as a series of adventures and experiments that were more serendipitous than carefully planned. 'When I graduated from LSE, I had heard how interesting and stimulating McKinsey was thought to be, so I focused on landing a job there. I was more opportunistic than deeply thoughtful about whether this was a great career step and certainly had no consciousness of how sought after a career option it turned out to be. I was extremely fortunate to get in,' she confides.

Anna's innate drive and willingness to put in the hard graft led to her doing well. One thing led to another, and opportunities followed.

'I think I may be the poster child for random career planning. I was opportunity led. The interesting thing is, I do think I realized I hadn't arrived yet. What I mean is, that I was on a journey of discovery. That I was trying different things on for size. Yes, I also needed to be pragmatic and make a living (especially as a largely single parent). I also wanted to be recognized as doing great work... of course. However, there was also this deeper restlessness to keep moving forward.'

Self-determination requires self-awareness

Anna says, as she looks back over her career, she realizes that she has one common thread. A cause, or purpose. She gains energy and feels great satisfaction in helping business leaders, executives, and other talented professionals be the best versions of themselves. She also talks effusively about the joy of working in teams and across networks.

'One of the things that defines me is this joy of working with teams and with others. I like the camaraderie. I gain something life-affirming from seeing others succeed. Ultimately, this may be my defining characteristic as an individual. I didn't really know that about myself at 23. All I knew was that I was unhappy. It took years of being willing to try new things, take some calculated risks, and, yes, recognize that I needed to define for myself what success feels like... not just take others' word for it! Mildly interesting too that I eagerly gave up the idea of attempting to become a "star" myself for helping others to fulfil themselves and bring that same commitment and sense of purpose to others.'

Careers tips

Anna talks about her career as a search for something elusive, combined with satisfying the immediate necessities demanded by life. 'My one big lesson is what I would describe as being constructively restless. It was more instinctive than planned. More organic than deliberate. But the outcome was

I seemed to naturally reinvent myself, proactively, every five to ten years.

'I do think your outlook, needs, and perspective changes with time. It's important not to settle or drift. In the end, life is more fun if you keep looking for what's next and taking calculated risks. I highly recommend the results. I've never been happier professionally than I am now. And I wouldn't be here if I'd settled along the way.'

Chapter 17

Professional Reinvention

How do you reinvent yourself? Why don't all of us manage to do this? Why is it so difficult? In this chapter we will explain why many of us struggle to adapt and change. Indeed, why many of us actively avoid it even when faced with seemingly overwhelming evidence that the consequence may be very bad for our careers, loved ones, health, and life.

Anyone who has been in the working world for any length of time will have experienced a change programme. Organizations are constantly shuffling their systems and processes. There are transformation programmes all over the place. Digitization of this. Streamlining of that. Consolidation of the other. There are small changes, like a new expense reimbursement system. Then there are major changes, like when your company announces it plans to cut 10,000 jobs. Change seems constant, relentless, everything, everywhere at the same time.

And yet, many corporate change initiatives fail. As many as 70% if you believe the most repeated statistic.[1] We shared the headlines on change programme success rates and their rather depressing statistics in our Introduction. The odds of success in a major change initiative look terrible until you consider the even longer odds we face as individuals. In some cases, the research suggests only 10% of us manage it.

So, how do we explain when the Elizabeth line was opened, there was a clamour to use it instead of the old Jubilee line.[2] When the latest gadget comes out from Apple, there are lines around the block to be the first to hold it, play with it. When we are young, we can't wait to be older. We reject our parents' admonishments to enjoy 'the best days of our lives'. Instead, we can't wait to drive a car, drink a beer, and make our own rules. We also celebrate and look forward to weddings, births, graduations. Our point is that there are some very consequential life changes that we seem to take in our stride.

How we relate to change is the key. New things we can add to our existing routines, that are our choice, we seem to enjoy. The acquisition of a desirable gadget can feel like a reward. The classic retail therapy dopamine hit. When we are given the choice to try a new train route, or fly on a new model of aeroplane, we see them as exciting adventures. While technically they are changes, we choose to relate to them as pleasant distractions. There are some distinctive characteristics to these sorts of changes. They aren't irrecoverable. We can choose to use the Elizabeth line today but go back to the Jubilee line tomorrow. Plus, they really don't disturb the fundamental pillars of our lives.

When it comes to more substantial, more seismic, irrevocable changes, they seem to come in two basic categories: (1) those we anticipate, plan for, and are carried on a wave of pervasive societal expectation, and (2) those that come as shocking, unwelcome surprises that we frame as deeply personal. Things like marriages, births, graduations, tend to fit into the first category. When we anticipate a big change, when our community, family, societal expectations are propelling us toward a big life event, we feel less threatened. Sure, there is trepidation, but there is a natural momentum that carries us toward them, through them, and to the other side. We feel like they are normal. They are, most importantly, celebrated as happy things.

In contrast, changes that we don't see coming, that are imposed upon us, feel very different. When you think about it, this happens at the more trivial end of the spectrum when our favourite coffee shop is unexpectedly closed, our plane is cancelled, or someone takes the vacant seat next to us even when the entire cabin is otherwise empty, then insists on having a conversation about the last election. In these cases, we experience irritation, frustration, even anger, albeit temporarily.

At the other end of the spectrum, when we are confronted with an unexpected, irrecoverable change that requires a massive, permanent, disruption to our routines, like our job, our work, our organization, our profession… we respond very differently. Analogous to the stages of grief. Initially, we vehemently resist it. We put every fibre of our being into denying it, avoiding it, delaying it, looking for an accommodation or work around. We wrack our brains for ways to turn back the clock, to attempt to find a way to unwind the change. It's so unfair, so unjust. Why now? What have we done to deserve this?

Why is unexpected seismic change so unwelcome?

Humans love routines. We spend our early lives striving to earn the right to live life on our terms. To do things our way. To organize our lives in a fashion that feels comfortable to us. This search for customization, for comfort, for routine, is completely natural.

What are routines other than a description of how we choose to live our lives. The outcome of years, decades, of trial and error. We come to embrace distinctive 'truths' about ourselves. We are early birds; we drink coffee, not tea; we like to exercise in the morning not evening; we prefer a window seat over the aisle; we eat healthily but allow ourselves an occasional treat. The thousands upon thousands of micro decisions that we make by the time we reach our 30s that are tailored, bespoke, to how we choose to live each day.

Routines help us run aspects of our lives on autopilot. They reduce our stress levels. They provide us with a sense of predictability that amplifies our sense of security. Indeed, routines can be the source of good health. Intuitively, this makes sense. You are probably nodding your head as you read this.

Neurological research supports your intuition. We mentioned the *basal ganglia* brain function in the previous chapter. This is responsible for helping us form and maintain routines. Once habits are programmed into our basal ganglia, they become harder to break. Our natural ageing process also has the effect of engraining routines deeper as we get older. As our brains mature, there is a natural moderation (we are avoiding the word diminishing) in our neural plasticity.[3] This results in us preferring continuity over change. There are also multiple studies that support the observations that as we age, we reduce our tolerance for adventure. Instead, we seek predictability.[4]

However, when we dig a little deeper, there are some other fascinating insights into how we behave when we get jolted. Neuroscientist Jaak Panksepp theorized that the paralysis, self-pity, and helplessness that we can experience is caused by one of our brain's seven systems being blocked: the SEEKING system.[5] This is similar to Sigmund Freud's concept of libido.[6] Our life force. Our enthusiasm to explore, search, or chase something. This is repressed when we suffer a shock. Our brain's systems go into a temporary panic.

When one views Panksepp's research in combination with the work of psychiatrist John Bowlby, the father of *attachment theory*, an even more vivid picture emerges of how we become deeply insecure and doubtful about ourselves immediately after we experience a surprise separation.[7] Like the death of a loved one or the loss of a job. Research by Cindy Hazan and Phillip Shaver has applied Bowlby's theories to professional life, concluding that most of us develop deep psychological attachments at work, sometimes unconsciously, even when we might outwardly wear badges of dispassionate detachment.[8]

The science consequently reinforces how we strive to find a comfortable routine and then jealously protect it. Our routines are profoundly important to us. They are our comfort blanket, our source of stability and security. Once we reach a professional equilibrium, we defend it like a parent defends their child. When something threatens it, we first seek to defend, protect, or avoid changing. But when the force disturbing us is irresistible, we enter a period of mourning. Our self-belief, our sense of adventure, our confidence, at least temporarily, evaporates. Leaving us feeling damaged, vulnerable, exposed.

Reflecting on Shey's experience in *Artificial Death of a Career*

When we wrote the murder mystery fable to accompany this book, we knew that the most realistic depiction of how Shey would experience the need for a major career reinvention was to tell a story of how he was unexpectedly ousted from FEEL VR. Shey finds himself flailing after Jian Xu tells him he is being replaced. The lead up to that moment is consciously veiled. We wanted to show that if you aren't paying careful attention, it's easy to misinterpret what's really going on. Many might say Shey was experiencing the epitome of a successful professional life. He was at the top of the tree. CEO of a unicorn AI start-up. However, if you looked deeper and follow as the story unfolds, you see that really wasn't the case.

Shey has a routine that he has embraced. He is in a bubble. He has found an equilibrium. But the truth is he isn't really moving. He's standing still. At work, he's leaning on El Gin to run the business and free himself from the stress of day-to-day business decisions. At home, in his personal life, he is also treading water. He hasn't moved forward in his romantic relationship. He has stood still while friends and family have moved on.

We wrapped the entire story in a murder mystery, because of the juxtaposition between how that signals, 'Hey, watch out… all is not what it seems in this story.' And that's the point. We stop thinking of our careers as a murder mystery, as a puzzle, as something that is in motion. Instead, we reach a point when we think to ourselves, 'OK… this feels comfortable. I think I've ticked off a bunch of things on my professional to-do list. I'm going to settle down now. Take it easy. Smell the flowers. Enjoy the view.'

What unfolds is Shey reacting predictably, with shock, anger, and denial when his routine is blown up. This is unfair he screams. Why me, he thinks. And – in the wallowing of self-pity, shame, and grief that follows – he projects his anger elsewhere. It must be someone else's fault. And so off he goes with Angelos to Shanghai, the LUD Club, and for his giraffe costume fitting.

At the end of the story, we set out two main questions: (1) Can we avoid sleepwalking toward obsolescence? And (2) If you want to reinvent your career, how do you do it?

Transition versus transformation

At this point in the chapter, we should probably come back and do a better job of defining what we mean by reinvention. When we are faced with a threat of extinction, the rational thing would be to make some fundamental changes in your professional trajectory. If you are a journalist witnessing more and more AI written content, it may be time to reimagine yourself as a different kind of writer. To consider other ways to think about purpose, cause, and explore alternative paths to be relevant and impactful.

The reality is quite different. Studies show that people who are made redundant in their middle careers are more likely to focus their efforts on securing a very similar position in another organization. As many as 70% in fact.[9,10] Our instincts when we are faced with an unexpected interruption in our careers is to move quickly to apply for similar jobs at other companies.

While some might suggest that whatever happens following a redundancy, severance, or exit from one company, might fit the broad description of reinvention, we think this isn't correct. After all, if you swap one corporate attorney job at company A for a very similar one at company B, your start and end points look very similar. Nothing has fundamentally changed about your profession, your job tasks, challenges, skills, attributes. Your pay, benefits, title might have changed slightly. In fact, it is commonly the place that we take a step down in all of these as we compromise our standards telling ourselves in the long run we will get back to where we started.[11]

We think the word **transition** is a better description for navigating a discontinuity in employment where there is no real change in career trajectory. This is very important in the context of our subject. If the world is changing, every day. If technology is eroding the foundations of decades-old professions. If companies are making rational decisions (give us some latitude on this point) about reducing jobs in areas that can be streamlined, made more efficient, and you find yourself caught in that net, well… aren't you swimming in an evaporating lake? Every time the music stops, won't there be fewer chairs? And won't the music stop more and more frequently?

Picking yourself up, dusting yourself off, and relaunching your career after a major knock back can be traumatic. Given everything we know about the psychology of identity, the profound sense of loss, of navigating grief, of repairing your sense of confidence and self-esteem, we in no way wish to diminish the scale of this challenge. There are some tremendous books that help those looking to navigate a job loss: *Rebound* by Martha Finney, *What Color is your Parachute* by Richard Bolles.[12,13] Although, we also recommend people read *Transitions* by William Bridges.[14]

A crisis of transition caused by an expected interruption in our careers can lead to feeling more defensive and conservative. We feel wounded. Consequently, we seek to quickly overcome the forced hiatus, and this fuels our sense that looking for something similar in another organization is the least line of resistance. Getting into action is part of us trying to heal ourselves. So, we make the search for a job, our job. We make a weekly calendar, set ourselves some goals, and update our résumé. We fire off 100 job applications via LinkedIn, network with our friends and ask them to keep us in mind. We do some industry research, contact some executive search firms and focus on promoting ourselves as best we can.

But is there an alternative? Is it completely impossible to think of a scenario where you get to much more proactively manage your career? Where you get to pre-emptively intervene? Where you remain vigilant, sensitive, and conscious of the opportunities and risks that are constantly reordering themselves around you? Maybe, we can avoid falling into the defensiveness that may follow an unexpected interruption. Instead, what would it look like for us to frame such an event as an opportunity, a blank slate? An opportunity for genuine introspection and reflection on where you are in your career, how the mega-trends of the moment are working to reshape the world of work and make a conscious calculation about how to re-align your own career strategy to ensure it remains relevant, fulfilling, necessary.[15] Given the choice, wouldn't you rather pursue a professional direction in an area that not only brought you a sense of fulfilment, but that also benefited from the 'tide raising boats' dynamic. Some professions are in decline. This has always been the case. But others are in their infancy. The old career order is being eroded and, in its place, beautiful new digital skyscrapers are emerging.

It's certainly possible. Statistically, about 30% of us do manage something more profound, more fundamental. Moreover, we make the case that anticipating and planning to substantially reduce the risk of being left standing in silence while all the old familiar chairs decay and disappear makes much more sense.

Reinvention versus transition

So, how do some people go through their careers without experiencing an unexpected unwelcome break? Where many of us fall into a trap of putting our professional lives on autopilot, and metaphorically sleepwalking towards a cliff of obsolescence, how do others avoid that fate?

In our story about Shey in *Artificial Death of a Career*, we focus on the consequences of allowing ourselves to drift. Our previous chapter addressed this subject in more detail and offered the **CAFFEINE** mnemonic to keep you wide awake to the risks of drift. Many of the components of the mnemonic are also effective devices for developing early warning signals. They represent a collective set of professional hacks that can help you act before you reach the edge of a professional relevance cliff.

However, they don't really address how some people don't need early warning signs. How some people seem continually restless, constantly curious, forever running toward something new. In pursuit of answering this question, we have spent time working with thousands of executives, coaching next generation talent, and working with entrepreneurs intent on changing the world. We have also looked at the careers of great thinkers and inventors like Thales of Miletus, da Vinci, Edison, Archimedes, Franklin, Pasteur, Fleming, and more recently Jobs, Gates, Bezos, and Branson.[16,17,18] Finally, we looked at people who have dedicated their lives to exploring, what we believe is a proxy for reinvention, such as Marco Polo, Columbus, Magellan, Cook, Scott, Amundsen, and, of course, Darwin.[19]

Our conclusion... there are four things that make these extraordinary people **TICK** (we can't help ourselves we know... and apologies for the artistic licence on the order). Four ingredients that seem to create a natural antidote to professional sleepwalking. They are:

1. **Knowing**: Self-awareness.
2. **Conviction**: Being driven by a strong belief, a cause, a sense of purpose.
3. **Impetus**: Always moving forward, striving, stretching, energetic.
4. **Toughness**: Resilience, perseverance.

Knowing

Perhaps this may surprise you. Often, we associate 'reality distortion fields' and 'cult of personalities' with the celebrated business leaders in our history. However, here we are not talking about the traits of conquerors, CEOs, or political leaders. We are talking instead of the qualities that underpin an ability to reinvent oneself.

In this context, possessing a healthy sense of who you are at your core is a foundational trait. Where denial, blindness, a wilful avoidance is rooted in a reluctance to confront realities, to come to terms with our own personal behaviours, our own role in conspiring to blow ourselves up, the reverse is true of those who embrace reinvention more intrinsically.

It makes complete sense when you pause to think about it. When we take the time to reflect and bring our unconscious actions to the fore, we are better able to recognize and adjust them. Having read this far, you will follow our assertion that much of the fault for falling victim of a career dead end lays with us. We are quick to blame others, assign colleagues, bosses, organizations with malintent. And, to some extent, perhaps there are unscrupulous people out there seeking to benefit from our demise. However, ask yourself the question, do we enable much of that? If we play the victim, are we offering ourselves up as easy targets?

We can all improve our self-awareness by taking simple steps; take a page from Uncle Freddy's teachings in *A Groundhog Career*, take time for reflection, keep a journal, ask questions, ask for feedback, give at least one person permission to call you out.[20]

Conviction

If self-awareness is the car we drive toward reinvention, then conviction is the fuel. In every single case of people who demonstrate the superpower of organic, intrinsic reinvention, they are passionate and clear sighted about a goal. Not a short-term goal like a new job, a promotion, or a pay rise, but a more overarching purpose. Something that we mentioned earlier that fits the *atelic* definition.[21]

In our research, we find it can be helpful to illustrate what we mean by cause. We point to the following examples.[22] Over the past 40 years, we have collected and consolidated down this list designed to illustrate and prompt discussion:

1. Change – fighting for change… righting a wrong… improving the world.
2. Love/Service – providing for or serving others.
3. Problem Solving – finding solutions to consequential problems.
4. Creation/Invention – pursuit of artistic expression, beauty.
5. Fellowship/Duty – *esprit de corps* and a sense of being needed.
6. Adventure – seeing how far you can go literally or metaphorically.

There are three things to bear in mind. The first is that they are situational. When you work through what you find compelling in your 20s, you will arrive at an answer that works for you at that time. As we have discussed, when you are in your 30s and 40s things change. You need to be careful not to assume that what excited you in your 20s will work for your entire life. It probably won't.

Second, it's OK if you struggle to find a cause or purpose initially. We sometimes draw a big circle around numbers three and six. Exploring life, careers, jobs, and problem solving, what that tells you about what fuels you can be its own purpose. In fact, we know some people, particularly in the Gen Z demographic, who are very much searching for something that they haven't yet found. Our advice is don't give up. By definition you will only find it if you put some effort into searching, experimenting, testing.

Finally, there are no rules on purpose. Your cause is yours. We have found that some people find revelation in unexpected places. Something as simple as 'belonging', feeling needed can be hugely powerful. Often, it is fighting to provide a better life for your family (here we do underline that families tend to grow up, creating an implicit need for reinvention). Occasionally, it's trying to change the world. Try not to make comparisons or assume your cause should fit some grandiose standard.

Impetus

How motivated are you? How energetic do you feel? Everyone gets tired at different times. However, what separates those who are very good at reinvention is that they are **constructively restless**. What we mean by this is that there is an instinct to associate boredom, energy depletion, as a trigger to make a change.

Having the drive to reinvent yourself is one of life's big challenges. When you read the research and the various books about professional reinvention, this question of knowing you should act but feeling unable to comes up time and time again. Sometimes it's described as laziness or procrastination.[23] Chip and Dan Heath in their book *Switch* refer to it more as having exhausted our capacity to change.[24] They promote the idea we can all change, but some of us have reached our emotional limits (which they call our *Elephants*). Their insight is instructive in that it helps us see how our overloaded emotional capacity can be drained by other aspects of our lives. They advance the idea that we must work to reduce that emotional load (*Finding the Path*) before we can move forward. In many ways, this sounds familiar, going back to the father of change theory Kurt Lewin and his *unfreeze, change, refreeze* hypothesis.[25]

There are some tricks to help in this space. The three we find most useful are:

1. **Succession**: Plan to move on from your current job every three years. When you commit to find your own replacement, it becomes a powerful reason for you to look forward toward what's next.

2. **Sabbaticals**: We associate the concept with academia and long breaks. However, we promote the idea that you can take a three- to four-week sabbatical in almost any job nowadays. We recommend you build this into your plan every three to five years. Find a remote mountain, a large ocean, a deserted island. Completely detach from your 'normal' life. Take your tote bag with assorted

books.[26] Keep a journal. Make yourself write down and justify, *why are you doing what you're doing, what's it all for*, and *where would you like to be in five to ten years and why?*

3. **Test the market**: When did you last test the job market? Do you know what your BATSQ (Best Alternative to Status Quo) is? What would you do if you weren't doing your current job? We recommend you do this once a year. Go and interview for one job. Find out what's out there. At best you'll reassure yourself you are on the right path. At worst, you'll realize something is wrong.

Toughness

Resilience is such an under-appreciated quality. All the people we have studied who prevail through good times and bad are able to weather professional storms. When we navigate dark periods in our professional lives, we widen our perspective. Bankruptcies, industrial accidents, terrorist assaults, evacuations from civil wars, mergers and acquisitions, unexpected and emotionally complex events.

The interesting thing is that once you've navigated one crisis you naturally build your resilience. Along the lines of the adage 'this too shall pass', or perhaps even more darkly 'if it doesn't kill you, it makes you stronger'. Perspective is a very powerful tool. When you've helped organize an evacuation from a war zone, you naturally become less tolerant of 'busy work'. When you attend the funeral for a colleague who was taken too soon, you think differently about what's important and what to stress about.

We recommend people volunteer to take on a crisis project. Some companies organize drills for pandemics, earthquakes, terrorist attacks. Some non-governmental organizations (NGOs) need volunteer help and advice. Put your hand up. Go along and see if you can help. In the process, we guarantee it will help you find new perspectives on your existing professional challenges.

Chapter reflection exercises

It is tempting to define ourselves by our vocational training. The danger is that these old professional labels can trap us in a backward-looking context. Accountant, lawyer, HR professional, journalist, manager may be widely understood job titles but if we wear them too restrictively they will ultimately starve our careers of oxygen. Reinvention requires us to discard these labels to instead think about how we contribute to what's next.

Challenge yourself to frame your future career path as being vital to one of the mega-trends reshaping the world of work. For example, how could you contribute to one of the following:

1. **Increasing knowledge transparency**. Technology is making information and knowledge easier to access. Can you frame your career as aggregating and leveraging disparate expertise to solve problems?

2. **New technology will demand new skills**. It's easy to focus on the jobs under threat from AI rather than the new jobs created. The World Economic Forum predict 97 million new AI jobs will be invented.[27] Are you focused on reshaping your career to serve one of these new work domains?

3. **Cybersecurity will be an increasingly existential threat**. Can you involve yourself in countering the threat?

4. **An ageing population will require new services.** Western economies will see an explosion in elderly care needs over the next 20 years.[28] Will you be part of a solution?

5. **Barriers to entrepreneurship will continue to lower.** Technology platforms will continue to create opportunities for Gen Z to test new business concepts more easily and at less up front cost.[29] Do you have your business plan drafted?

6. **Sustainable energy will be paramount.** We hear a lot about data being the new gold, so perhaps sustainable energy is the new oxygen. The latest technology only works when plugged in. Are you working to help solve this problem?

7. **Humans will seek new ways to be entertained.** There is a lighter side to the darkness some predict about technology. Humans are incredibly good at finding new ways to have fun.

This isn't an exhaustive list but provides a good prompt to help you try to escape legacy labels and think about how you make sure your career benefits from a rising tide.

Chapter blink

- Reinvention and seismic personal change are difficult.

- However, we easily navigate some big life changes when we can anticipate them, and our context makes it feel like something to be celebrated.

- The scientific research reinforces how we like routines and are very reluctant to change them.

- When we are blindsided by a redundancy or major work change, we go through stages of grief.

- **Transition** is often something we choose over **reinvention**.

- The **CAFFEINE** mnemonic can help us set up early warnings that unexpected change is on the horizon.

- We know how the people who instinctively and proactively reinvent their careers **TICK**:

  - **Know themselves** – they are good at introspection.

  - **Conviction** – they hold a strong conviction about what they do.

- **Impetus** – they have the energy to pursue new horizons.

- **Toughness** – they are resilient and have a great perspective on what's important.

• Set yourself the challenge to be relevant in the context of today's career mega-trends.

In three phrases

1. **Anticipate Change** – we are better when we can see change coming.

2. **Routine Can Be Your Ruin** – recognize your affection for status quo.

3. **Tick Tick... No Boom** – build your reinvention skills. They will help you avoid unexpected explosions.

Dr Anand Verma
Serial entrepreneur, AI trailblazer and climate visionary

Anand's story begins in an industrial city of Jamshedpur in India, born as the youngest of five to value driven but modest parents. His story sounds like a movie script, gripping yet real and inspiring. His career journey starts long before coming to England. It starts with big dreams in a society with strict societal boundaries. His supportive parents instilled in him the value of education, hard work and big dreams as the most likely way to a better and more promising life. In this spirit Anand fearlessly founded companies, sold them, scaled them and always chose new challenges over the more stable and predictable corporate executive alternative.

My career and life story

As JRD Tata wisely observed, 'The purpose of an organization is to enable ordinary people to do extraordinary things.'

'My unusual and almost dreamlike journey is a testament to the power of resilience, determination, and believing in one's ability to create meaningful change. Growing up as the youngest in a family of five, I experienced first-hand the challenges of modest circumstances. Our daily struggle was real – sometimes there wasn't enough food on the table. Yet, my parents' and my eldest brother's unwavering commitment was clear: education for all was our pathway to a better future.

'The society I grew up in was restrictive, often limiting dreams and potential. But limitations became my motivation. I was creative, sporty, hardworking and a go-getter. At 19, I took a leap of faith that would define my entire professional trajectory. With just £100 in my pocket and a scholarship to the UK, I embarked on a journey of self-discovery and survival.'

The secret to success is discipline, hard work and pushing beyond limiting beliefs

'Those early days were a crucible of character formation. Surviving meant working multiple jobs, relying entirely on myself. I learned quickly that resilience isn't just about enduring; it's about adapting rapidly and pushing beyond perceived limitations. Each challenge was a lesson, each obstacle an opportunity. I actually became a founder at the university by helping students type their assignments for £20 a pop. Fun fact: I met my wife at the university and she has been the biggest cheerleader throughout. My first start-up experience in the late '90s was a rollercoaster. We were passionate, committed, and ultimately caught in the dot-com crash. Many would have seen this as a defeat, but for me, it was a great learning experience.

'As my career progressed, I became one of the youngest presidents in a global media tech company. It was a prestigious position with an enviable salary, but something was missing. I realized that true fulfilment comes not from titles or compensation, but from creating genuine, impactful solutions.'

Business is about pushing boundaries and continuous reinvention

'In 2012, I took another leap. I founded my second start-up focused on world class UX and Design that could genuinely improve people's lives. This wasn't just about business; it was about "teaching elephants to dance" – challenging established systems and creating meaningful change by putting users at the heart of their organizations. We were solving real problems while maintaining a holistic approach that considered people, planet, and profit. I was lucky enough to exit that company to create an even bigger impact.

'Today, as the founder and CEO of Expect AI, I continue this mission of purposeful innovation. Our focus is leveraging AI to help businesses boost their margins while simultaneously driving sustainable initiatives. It's a delicate balance of economic pragmatism and sustainability.

'My core philosophy remains unchanged: take risks, commit fully, and work relentlessly towards creating meaningful impact. While corporate structures often constrain innovation, start-ups offer a mission-oriented approach that allows genuine measurable transformation and now even more rapidly with the power of generative AI.'

Business isn't personal but succeeding is

'We are all shaped by our beginnings. My burning desire to succeed was in part due to the context I experienced in my youth. I held an unwavering conviction that I needed to succeed. I didn't question obstacles or setbacks. I didn't lament them or see them as unfair. I used them as learnings or opportunities to refocus. As the famous NASA line goes "mission failure was not an option".

'However, at some stage the initial burning fire must transition into something else. Less instinctive and more deliberate and conscious. In my case, I have found that when you are constantly looking to the future, when you have a fascination for the next new thing, it creates its own antidote to obsolescence. Equally, where my youthful verve to succeed may have been replaced by this ever-present enthusiasm to explore new boundaries, I have never lost sight that business is the ultimate scorecard for both long-term purpose and profit. It isn't sentimental. It rewards good ideas and great execution and punishes the reverse. For me, this realistic view of business with purpose has served me very well. Ultimately, you must take accountability for your own success.'

Career tips

'To young professionals and aspiring entrepreneurs, I offer this wisdom: your background does not define your potential. Resilience is not about never falling but about rising every time you fall. Embrace challenges, stay curious, and never stop believing in your capacity to create change.

'My journey proves that with grit, obsession, and a commitment to purpose, you can turn modest beginnings into extraordinary achievements.'

Chapter 18

Business Reality 101

'*The board met this morning and have decided to appoint a new CEO – effective immediately.*' These are the words of chairman Jian in his conversation with Shey – unwavering, uncompromising with no room for interpretation or negotiation. Deep inside, Shey knew something was not right; his intuition had warned him of choppy water ahead. He picked up on the spontaneous nature of the conversation, the tone of Jian's voice, and his own nervousness.

Jian attempted to soften the news for Shey, saying that it was nothing personal, only business. But that didn't make it any easier. In fact, the lack of emotion made it worse. For a founder/CEO, calling it 'just business' is a slap in the face. For every founder, business is purpose, and purpose becomes an all-consuming way of life – for better or worse.

One of our goals with this book is to shine a light on how business' essential realities sometimes feel individually unfair. Something we emphasize in *Artificial Death of a Career*. There is a temptation for individuals to believe they are owed something beyond what fundamental capitalist principles demand. We explain this as individuals grappling with how they are treated in the business world and how that sometimes feels jarring with their sense of fairness and individual justice (there is a whole field of research established by the American moral philosopher John Rawls on this subject).[1] Our overarching point is that Shey's sense of 'injustice' is anchored in distorted beliefs about what the business world owes any one individual.

In this chapter, we will look at this point while also attempting to demystify the essential ingredients for entrepreneurial success. What we have titled **Business Reality 101**. It won't go into the intricacies of micro- or macro-economics. We will leave out the Harvard case studies, and steer clear of the Michael Porter lectures. This chapter explores the essential realities of business; the fundamental truths that have held true since the emergence of capitalism as the world's dominant economic system. Our focus will be on new businesses, on start-ups, and on the mindset and attitude necessary to become or be a good founder and/or CEO. Some people can become brilliant founder/CEOs, but most will not.

To succeed requires being anchored in the essential realities of capitalist fundamental principles, along with some key personal attributes – timing, patience, persistence, and constant reinvention. And, for some, most importantly, it is about knowing when to take yourself out of the business: everything and everyone has an expiry date. In today's world, originality of thought, being able to be a contrarian, and having the courage to explore new paths is important.

We believe succeeding in business requires a great awareness of timing. There is as much art as there is science in business. Our metaphor for the artistic component is a symphony... and to succeed you need the timing of a good (if not maestro) conductor. In this vein, we have structured this chapter in five movements:

- **Movement 1:** 'The essence of business over time' explores seminal moments in the history and evolution of business. We aim to draw out eternal principles with timeless value.
- **Movement 2:** This is a deep dive into the distinctive phenomenon of start-ups, examining what makes them successful. We will also relate back to some of the business principles that have been successful since the Industrial Revolution.
- **Movement 3:** This explores why most start-ups fail and what can be learned from these failures.
- **Movement 4:** What does business owe you personally? Here we explore the juxtaposition between achieving shareholder priorities and collateral damage.
- **Movement 5:** Summarizes the above learnings to provide handrails and the dos and don'ts of good business.

Movement 1: 'The essence of business over time', seminal thinking and literature – what really matters

Much has been written about business, leadership, breakthroughs, and ingredients for success. Every month we have an endless stream of articles from McKinsey, HBR, and others in our inbox. Often, the popular fads have short shelf lives. Each year they are replaced by a new headline, and a new wave of consulting initiatives are launched. It can be a daunting and confusing challenge to resist getting swept along with each wave... falling into the trap of being busy but not productive. Much of what is written also reinforces urban myths, things that are not always what they first appear. The challenge is sorting the wheat from the chaff. Many successful entrepreneurs attest to the importance of reading, to broaden one's horizon and get inspiration, but simple reading isn't sufficient – developing a sceptical filter is also important.

A few years ago, an article in *Inc* caught our attention. It stated that three universities (Stanford, Harvard, and Berkeley) produced 90% of US unicorns.[2] It also contradicted the belief many people hold that university dropouts are better founders. Yes, Bill Gates, Steve Jobs, and Mark Zuckerberg didn't complete their degrees, but the majority of great founders did. Regardless of whether they ever wore a cap and gown, successful founders have three things in common: they use a critical eye, think deeply, and act fast.

We have distilled here some critical areas of thought inspired by books, articles, podcasts, and plenty of practical experience. Here you will gain insights that are useful for business and life without having to go through the tedious process of reading hundreds of books. We highlight six thought leaders, starting with Frederick Winslow Taylor and his thoughts on industrial production, then move to Chester Irving Barnard who wrote about the role of executives. Taylor and Barnard represent the start of the 20th century. We then turn to Theodore Levitt's theory about the importance of customer focus, a key *Harvard Business Review* article from the second of half to the 20th century, and then Jim

Collins, a favourite of ours, who we believe revolutionized business literature in the late 20th century. Then we touch on Erik Ries and his theory on successful start-ups before concluding with the champion of capitalism Milton Friedman. Friedman provides the perfect punctuation and inspiration for our oft-repeated phrase 'it's not personal... it's only business.'

A brief history of business theory

The late 19th and early 20th centuries were foundational in shaping modern business thought. During this period, the focus was on establishing approaches to management and understanding the complexities of industrial production and enterprises. *The Principles of Scientific Management* by Frederick Winslow Taylor (1911) is the first book we want to single out.[3] It is a compact text and easy to read. Taylor was a mechanical engineer who worked in manufacturing but later became a business consultant. The foundational thinking of Taylorism is that the systematic study of tasks or processes can lead to significant productivity improvements and that standardization is crucial for operational efficiency. These two ideas remain relevant more than a hundred years later. In our corporate and non-corporate experience, we have seen these simple principles disregarded by both small start-ups and large mega-corporations time and again.

Another thought leader in this space is Chester Irving Barnard. His book, *The Functions of Executive* (1938), for us, contains two relevant themes for today: organizations function as co-operative systems, requiring effective communication, and that the informal networks play a vital role in achieving formal organizational goals.[4] Understanding this affords a good explanation for why so many organizations fail and why so few companies thrive over a long period of time. We have worked with centennial organizations (for-profit and non-governmental organizations (NGOs)) as well as organizations that failed spectacularly. This practical experience has shaped our thinking and perception of business just as much as our studies. It has helped us enormously to understand what it takes to build businesses and careers that last.

From studying Barnard's work and our own business experience, we believe there are two main leadership styles to choose from: to lead in an authoritative way or to lead in an inclusive, engaging way. Ideally, a hybrid model with a wide toolkit is the best way to succeed. After all, some people and situations need carrots, while others need sticks.

In a 1960 *Harvard Business Review* article, 'Marketing Myopia', the economist Theodore Levitt identified an important reason for why so many companies fail: they focus too much on selling products rather than on what the customer needs.[5] Levitt said that businesses must focus on solving customer problems and satisfying their needs. He also highlighted the importance of fostering innovation and building sustainable businesses.

Turning to more recent writing, Jim Collins' *Good to Great: Why some companies make the leap... and others don't* (2001) introduces concepts such as Level 5 Leadership, emphasizing the importance of discipline, thought, and action, and also humility.[6] Collins cautions that intrinsic motivation is far more important than a big ego, that greatness is not a function of circumstances, it is a function of choice.

What the above examples demonstrate is a need to be aware and to learn while you develop your business. This a tenet of *The Lean Startup: How Today's Entrepreneurs Use Continuous Innovation to Create Radically Successful Businesses* (2011) by Eric Ries, in which the key message is that the only way to win is to learn and improve faster than anyone else.[7]

Finally, a short discussion on the realities of what capitalist business is and isn't wouldn't be complete without some reference to Milton Friedman.[8] The *Friedman Doctrine* simply emphasizes the primacy of shareholder value. The bedrock of the capitalist system, its ultimate purpose, is to return value to investors. This primacy remains inescapable. Yes, there have been attempts to temper and qualify it. To suggest that it is moderated by social good, regulation, individual, and workers' rights. However, the stark reality is that any business that loses sight of it gets into trouble very quickly. Therefore, Friedman helps underscore rule number one in business – *satisfy shareholders*.

This list is not exhaustive but is a great starting point for the non-academic, risk taking, and action-oriented leader and entrepreneur to develop their thinking and pathway to success. We deliberately haven't mentioned management consultant and author Peter Drucker, but he is a must-read for everyone, as his books have a timeless relevance.

Movement 2: The magic of success – analysis of successful start-ups, what went right

Let's now explore practical insights for those who aspire to build or lead successful ventures. The media focus on success stories may provide a distorted view that many start-up stories seem effortless. The reality is very different. Every start-up faces almost daily hard lessons, near-failures, and moments where things could easily have fallen apart. Below are three start-ups that transformed their industries and, in the process, teach us something about the essence of business.

1. Revolut: Revolutionizing fintech

In 2015, Nikolay Storonsky, a frustrated investment banker, decided to tackle one of the most persistent problems in finance: exorbitant fees for currency exchange and international transactions.[9] Revolut launched with a simple idea – an app-based financial service that would allow customers to spend and transfer money globally with minimal fees.

What went right

Revolut's success wasn't just about its innovative product; it was about timing and execution. The world was ready for a disruption in traditional banking, and Revolut seized the moment. Storonsky's relentless focus on solving customer pain points – transparency, ease of use, and cost efficiency – built trust and loyalty.

But Revolut didn't stop at one feature. It expanded into cryptocurrencies, stock trading and business accounts, becoming a financial super-app for individuals and companies.

Key insight

Timing is everything. Revolut entered the market just as fintech was gaining traction, and its customer-centric approach allowed it to scale rapidly. The lesson? Solve a real problem first, then evolve to meet your customers' next needs.

2. Gymshark: Building a brand, not just a business

Ben Francis didn't set out to create a global fitness empire.[10] In 2012, he was a teenager selling fitness supplements and gym apparel from his parents' garage while working part time as a delivery driver. Fast forward to today and Gymshark is a billion-dollar brand. What's the secret?

What went right

Gymshark didn't just sell clothing; it sold a lifestyle. Francis understood the power of community before it became a buzzword. By partnering with fitness influencers, Gymshark created an aspirational but accessible brand. People didn't just buy gym wear – they became part of the Gymshark movement.

Crucially, Francis embraced mistakes early on. When his initial suppliers failed to deliver quality products, he took production in-house. This move not only ensured better quality but also gave Gymshark control over its brand identity.

Key insight

The best brands are more than products; they're cultural movements. By building a community-first approach, Gymshark turned customers into advocates and influencers into brand ambassadors.

3. Meta (formerly Facebook): From dorm room to dominance

No analysis of successful start-ups is complete without mentioning Meta.[11] What started as a college project in 2004 has grown into one of the most influential companies in history. But Meta's success wasn't a straight line – it is a story of constant reinvention.

What went right

From day one, Mark Zuckerberg understood the power of networks. Facebook's ability to grow through user connections created a snowball effect – each new user made the platform more valuable. But its real strength lay in Zuckerberg's willingness to disrupt his own business model.

The acquisitions of Instagram and WhatsApp were transformative, as was the pivot towards the metaverse. Meta's trajectory shows that great companies don't just adapt to change – they anticipate it.

Key insight

Growth isn't just about scale, it's about reinvention. The willingness to disrupt yourself can be the difference between short-term success and long-term dominance.

Movement 3: Analysis of some unsuccessful start-ups, what went wrong

Here we offer practical insights into what can go and has gone wrong for start-ups. The previous section show-cased the thrilling landscape of innovation, risk, resil-ience, and huge success. Yet the harsh reality is that most start-ups never make it to the top.

A number of studies show that only about 20–30% of start-ups are still operational after ten years.[12] For many, the road to longevity is fraught with challenges, from funding woes to market missteps. Even for those that achieve the coveted 'unicorn' status – a valuation exceeding $1 billion – the odds of sustained success are sobering. As of recent reports, less than 1% of start-ups worldwide reach unicorn status, and among them, nearly 20% fail within just three years.[13]

These numbers highlight that even extraordinary growth does not guarantee long-term viability. The allure of start-ups often masks their precariousness. Even those backed by millions or billions in capital are not immune to collapse. Take Jawbone, a promising unicorn that fell apart due to mismanagement and cash flow issues.[14] Tutorspree succumbed to scalability despite early promise.[15] The most prominent failure of all is Theranos, which after a meteoric rise ended in fraud allegations, leaving behind a cautionary tale about ambition without accountability and integrity.[16]

Let's take a closer look at what went wrong.

1. Jawbone: The perils of overreach

Once a darling of Silicon Valley, Jawbone began with Bluetooth headsets and speakers before pivoting to wearables. The company raised more than $900 million in funding and was valued at $3 billion at its peak. But despite its promise, Jawbone fell apart in 2017.

What went wrong

Jawbone tried to do too much too quickly. Its foray into wearables came at a time when competition from Fitbit and Apple was heating up. The company struggled with product delays, technical failures, and poor customer service. Worse, it burned through cash without achieving profitability.

Key insight

Focus is critical. Jawbone's downfall reminds us that ambition must be matched by execution. Trying to dominate multiple categories without a clear strategy can lead to overextension – and failure.

2. Tutorspree: A great idea without a market

Tutorspree aimed to connect students with tutors, like an Airbnb for education. The idea was compelling, and the platform saw early traction. Yet, it shut down after just three years.

What went wrong

Tutorspree's model was operationally clunky and difficult to scale. Unlike Airbnb, where listings are static, tutoring required constant matchmaking and support. Additionally, demand wasn't as high or consistent as the founders anticipated. Tutorspree also faced stiff competition from larger, better-funded platforms.

Key insight

Even the best ideas need a scalable market. Tutorspree's failure underscores the importance of validating demand and ensuring operational efficiency.

3. Theranos: The dark side of ambition

No discussion of start-up failures is complete without Theranos. Promising revolutionary blood-testing technology, Elizabeth Holmes captivated investors raising nearly $1 billion. But the technology didn't work, and the company's practices were riddled with deception.

What went wrong:

Theranos didn't just fail; it imploded. The obsession with secrecy, the toxic culture of fear, and Holmes' refusal to admit flaws created an ethical and operational disaster. While many start-ups fake it until they make it,

Theranos crossed the line – endangering lives and eroding public trust.

Key insight

Ethics and transparency aren't optional. In the start-up world, credibility is currency and losing it can lead to irreparable damage.

Breakdowns and breakthroughs

What separates Revolut, Gymshark, and Meta from Jawbone, Tutorspree, and Theranos? Often, it is the ability to turn a breakdown into a breakthrough. Successful start-ups face their crises head-on – using them as opportunities to adapt, innovate, and rebuild.

- Revolut navigated regulatory scrutiny to strengthen its compliance systems.
- Gymshark learned from production setbacks to take control of its supply chain.
- Meta faced reputational challenges and used them to evolve its business model.

In contrast, failed start-ups ignored warning signs, clung to flawed strategies, or let ambition overshadow reality.

Movement 4: Becoming collateral damage

YouTube and TikTok seem to have countless examples of people caught in the seemingly callous net of corporate 'rightsizing'. There was a viral video of the person laid off over video by Crowdstrike.[17] There was also furore following the news that the CEO of Better.com, a mortgage unicorn start-up announced he would lay off 15% of the workforce… via a Zoom call. This was aggravated by his firm having just received a cash infusion of $750 million.[18] The resulting uproar tells us something about society's expectations. About how we are quick to paint corporations as uncaring and shameless. There is a bias to side with the worker. Why is that?

The simple explanation is that we can empathize with an individual. It's much harder to do that with an organization. We have also been fed a steady diet of stories to reinforce an image of businesses as the bad actors.[19] Jill Brown has done research into this, citing the media's portrayal of corporate greed and malevolence from Enron to the Wall Street banks, through oil companies, and including the recent coverage of FTX, Theranos, and WeWork.[20] When you add to that organized labour's repeated narrative of business leadership as uncaring mercenaries or 'fat cats', it shouldn't be too much of a surprise that we tend to champion individuals over corporations.[21]

In Shey's case, he is fired by Jian. Shey's instinct is to feel victimized. To personalize the decision. As we have mentioned earlier, this is never more acute than in the case of a founder who finds themselves in a power struggle. It is perhaps more akin to a custody battle or divorce than some unemotional objective and logical calculation. What could possibly be more personal than being told what you have dedicated yourself to is being 'stolen' away? Ultimately, however, the world of business, and in particular the capitalist invention of corporations, follow only one 'golden' rule: *satisfy the shareholders.*

Where the *Freidman Doctrine* meets individual justice, shareholders' interests break any ties. This is easy in extreme cases. For example, faced with the decision to go bankrupt and lose 10,000 jobs, you can instead make 1,000 redundant and save the company. In the abstract, this seems to make perfect utilitarian sense. Unless you are one of the 1,000. If you are a great performer, have given ten years of your life to a company, never put a foot wrong, never taken all of your vacation, worked overtime without being asked, volunteered for special projects... How is it fair for you to be rewarded with a severance package?

The answer is that it isn't. They are false equivalences. They aren't true alternatives. One may be a consequence of the other. However, it is unrealistic to expect a company with the choice in the prior paragraph to place individual justice for all 1,000 ahead of the viability of the entire business.

So, the real point here for individuals is to be realistic when it comes to career choices, organizational loyalty, longevity, and expectations. In our experience, it should be reasonable to expect:

- **Authenticity**: Being treated like an adult when it comes to your organization's plans.
- **Transparency**: About how difficult decisions are going to be made. We have specifically chosen this word over fairness. Fairness is subjective.

There are some good frameworks provided by the CIPD, SHRM, and ACAS on how best to make downsizing decisions. However, if you are selected for redundancy, it's understandable that you may feel unfairly treated.

- **Respectfulness**: Above all else, the one ever present should be the expectation of being dealt with respectfully. The examples we gave earlier of Crowdstrike and Better.Com are good 'not to' examples.

However, where the golden rule for business is satisfying shareholders, the bigger lesson here is that for you as an individual, the golden rule really should be to take primary responsibility for driving your career. Make informed, risk-adjusted decisions on how best to achieve your professional goals. Sometimes, this will mean you need to anticipate bumps in the road and trust your own judgement on what is best for you.

Movement 5: Handrails for success – the dos and don'ts

Here we summarize the most relevant take-aways from this chapter. Today, finding professional success for leaders in their 30s, like our protagonist Shey, requires more than just ambition. It demands a disciplined approach to decision making, a willingness to learn from history, and an ability to anticipate and proactively take responsibility to reinvent yourself.

Below are actionable insights for success, a framework to help you lead with pragmatism, insight, and resilience. We have four key handrails for success that we have found useful over the years and have never failed us:

- Think – Speak – Do, in that order.
- When hiring or surrounding yourself with people, take time, find the best. IQ-EQ-DRIVE are key, but attitude and integrity are everything.
- Never give up, perseverance is everything, failure is part of it and a great of way of learning, but make sure that you have one person in your life that you allow to be a mirror.
- Look after yourself, nobody is more interested in your wellbeing and success than you are.

The Dos: Building resilience and agility

1. Think deep, act fast
   As highlighted in Movement 1, the best leaders combine thoughtful analysis with decisive action. Avoid being paralyzed by overthinking; instead, focus on informed, swift decisions that keep you ahead of the curve.
2. Focus on the customer, not the product
   From Theodore Levitt's 'Marketing Myopia' to Revolut's journey, the message is clear: businesses succeed when they solve real customer problems. Engage deeply with your audience to understand their evolving needs and innovate to meet them.

3. Embrace adaptability and anticipate road bumps
   Success stories like Meta and Gymshark show that reinvention is a cornerstone of longevity. Be willing to disrupt your own business model and embrace change as an opportunity rather than a threat.

4. Leverage informal networks
   Chester Irving Barnard emphasized the power of informal organizations to achieving goals. Foster trust and collaboration within your teams, creating an environment where innovation thrives.

5. Learn fast, fail smarter
   Eric Ries' lean start-up model underscores the importance of rapid iteration and learning. Treat failures as valuable feedback, using them to refine your strategy and product.

6. Invest in culture and community
   Gymshark's community-first approach demonstrates the value of building emotional connections with your audience. Internally, create a culture of accountability, transparency, and inclusivity to drive long-term engagement and loyalty.

7. Sustainability as strategy
   Businesses that prioritize sustainability, both environmental and operational, build resilience against future shocks. Innovate with a mindset towards sustainable growth to create enduring value.

The don'ts: Avoiding pitfalls

1. **Don't overextend**
    Jawbone's downfall is a cautionary tale of doing too much, too soon. Focus on core strengths before diversifying, ensuring that every expansion is strategic and sustainable.

2. **Don't ignore warning signs**
    Start-ups such as Theranos failed because they overlooked critical flaws and operated in denial. Regularly audit your business processes, seeking feedback from both internal and external stakeholders.

3. **Don't prioritize ego over mission**
    Jim Collins' concept of Level 5 Leadership highlights the dangers of egocentric decision making. Lead with humility, prioritizing the mission and team over personal recognition.

4. **Don't neglect ethics and transparency**
    The Theranos debacle shows that cutting ethical corners erodes trust and credibility. Build transparency into your operations and maintain accountability to stakeholders at every level.

5. **Don't chase trends without strategy**
    Avoid the temptation to follow fleeting market trends without alignment to your long-term vision. Stay grounded in your mission and pivot strategically, not reactively.

6. **Don't fall foul to blind faith**
    And finally, try not to get caught as an innocent victim of business cycles. Take personal

responsibility for weighing the risks in your career, with your job, and look critically at the information you are being given. If it doesn't add up, look for something else.

While we value research and examples, anyone who has worked with us knows that we love quizzes. So, below we have a quick quiz challenge. We haven't provided the answers but encourage you to find your own answers and conclusions. If you need help or context, contact us via our website.

1. How much is 19 × 27? You have 15 seconds.
2. How many start-ups fail and how many make it to unicorn status?
3. What educational background have most successful founders?
4. What is the Y-combinator and what is its significance?
5. Why is London a good place for a start-up in Europe?
6. Fake it until you make it – agree or disagree?

Final insight and chapter closing reflection: Lead with purpose

In the end, business success is about more than profits and valuations. It's about creating lasting value for customers, empowering your team, and contributing positively to the world. The best leaders don't just build companies – they build legacies.

As you navigate the complexities of leadership, let these handrails guide you. Stay focused, stay adaptable, and remember greatness is not a function of circumstance but a function of choice. Our hero Shey did many things right but got one thing wrong: he didn't realize he was bored, and the complexities of his adult life took his toll. He increasingly lived in a bubble. Being fired can be a gift!

Chapter blink

- The golden rule of capitalism is SATISFY SHAREHOLDERS.

- The cornerstones of successful business strategy are solving a real customer problem, being bold, innovating constantly, and leveraging technology in new ways.

- A great business strategy means little without effective organization, planning, and self-aware leadership.

- It's all about people – the greatest leaders are always talent scouting. Invest in founders not products.

- The big traps are losing focus, becoming stale, ethical implosions, and not achieving scale.

- Self-belief and self-confidence are important; however, a good, long, and self-critical look in the mirror goes a long way. Humility and intrinsic motivation eat ego for breakfast.

- Ownership mindset will make you stand out when you are employed. It's a rare mindset in large companies.

- It's not personal – take responsibility for your professional future. Nobody is more interested in your wellbeing and success than you are!

In three phrases

- **Clarity and Focus** – discipline and efficiency will always matter. Find ways to stay alert and agile.

- **Failure is Part of Success** – it's a result of deep thought, speed, and perseverance. Recognize that you need to be smarter, faster, and more pragmatic than others.

- **Attitude is Everything** – only work with people with integrity, a good brain, and good work ethics.

Peter Tauchner-Hoover
Professional Tennis Player to Wealth Manager

'I loved playing sport. During my childhood and early adulthood, I was obsessed with tennis. I immersed myself in it. It was all I thought about. And in many respects, it taught me some valuable lessons about succeeding in life.

'There's a German saying that translates roughly to "playing sports is a school for life". Sports taught me discipline, the immense power of mindset on performance, and the realization that many of our self-imposed limitations are just illusions. Tennis also instilled in me the belief that life is a meritocracy: your success or failure depends on you and you alone. If you want to achieve something, it's your responsibility to make it happen.

'When it came time to choose a profession beyond tennis, I was initially unsure. The world was still recovering from the great financial crisis, and headlines about how capital markets should work caught my attention. It reminded me of my grandfather, who used to analyze stock prices on teletext to decide his next investment move. His methodical approach and competitive spirit resonated with me. The more I learned about finance, the more I was drawn to its meritocratic nature – where success is measurable, often by the P&L you generate.

'The idea of "keeping score" felt like a natural extension of the competitive drive that had served me well in sports.

'I also appreciated the field's objectivity. As someone who wasn't naturally extroverted, I liked the idea of a career where performance could be measured by tangible outcomes rather than subjective opinions. This led me to pursue a role in the markets division of a large bank, where I was fortunate to secure a spot in their graduate programme. I entered the workforce with the same mindset I had on the tennis court: outperform the competition, and you'll advance to the next round.

'And so my career took off. I did really well... until I didn't.

'The competitive and disciplined mindset I leaned on did propel me in the hyper-competitive, highly quantitative world of finance. But it did leave me vulnerable to two things I didn't fully appreciate, which rather took me by surprise.

'The first is that my approach was a bit one dimensional. I was missing out on the broader qualitative aspects of life. I had a dim recollection of my mother telling me that all work made for a humdrum existence. I'm not sure I fully appreciated what that really meant until I experienced a sense of loneliness. A nagging doubt that despite my professional success, I was missing out on experiencing all that life had to offer. Perhaps like many others I dismissed the nagging doubts for probably longer than I should. All that changed when I unexpectedly met my wife.

'As things started to fall into place in my career, my life felt like it was on cruise control – until something unexpected happened.

'I say *unexpected,* because before meeting her, I had never envisioned having a life partner, let alone being married. I loved the freedom to focus on work, travel, or move to a new country on a whim for a job opportunity. While I understood the positives of having someone to share life with, I worried that a long-term relationship might force me to choose between my career and personal life. Tennis had taught me that you must make sacrifices to succeed.

'I couldn't have been more wrong. My wife, far more extroverted and empathetic than I am, not only made me a better person but also helped me make strides in my career. By that point, I had developed a more holistic view of my company, but I still struggled to understand what truly motivated others and how to adapt my approach to bring out their best. Her natural empathy helped me bridge that gap, teaching me that collaboration is as much about understanding people as it is about sharing goals. Perhaps as importantly, I learned to relax, to explore other pastimes, to embrace aspects of life that I had overlooked.

'The second thing that surprised me was how I assumed my network, my family, my support system was constant. Again, using my tennis training, there are assumptions about coaching, physiotherapy, and conditioning. You rely on the support team. You climb on their shoulders every time you win. Equally, they pick you up when you suffer a tough loss.

'When I think of my early professional life, I was consumed by building my career for many years. I didn't pay enough attention to how my personal support team was ageing, becoming distracted, moving gradually away from me.

'A big professional life lesson for me is that being focused, committed, and ambitious is essential to succeed. But it's important not to confuse those traits with being insular, disconnected, and self-absorbed. We succeed, in the long run, with the help of others.

'Moreover, the fundamental point of a career is to share the benefits, share the rewards with people who matter. You must keep that in mind and make sure you embrace, not avoid, the complexity of adult life.

'I think there's a lot of truth in the saying "playing sports is a school for life." But I would add one more lesson: "Life is a team sport."'

Chapter 19

Surfing the Complexity of Adult Life

We love *The Brady Bunch*, the TV sitcom created in the late 1960s.[1] It wasn't particularly successful during its initial run but became an evergreen stalwart. Even today, teenagers love to watch reruns. Why is it relevant for us here? *The Brady Bunch* writers had a keen and under-appreciated eye for the realities of family life. As Mark Twain memorably quipped: 'Laughter without a tinge of philosophy is but a sneeze of humour. Genuine humour is replete with wisdom.'[2]

A wonderful illustration of Twain's observation, *The Brady Bunch* provides a cultural dramatization for navigating the complexities of adult life, with humour, optimism amongst the messy realities of blending two households into one. Debuting in 1969, the show follows the union of Carol and Mike Brady, each bringing three children into a single home – a microcosm of 1970s idealism. However, beneath its sunny veneer and catchy theme song lies a story that resonates deeply because it grapples with timeless questions: how do we mix identities, responsibilities, and individual dreams into a cohesive supporting unit?

The appeal of *The Brady Bunch* endures not just because of its nostalgic value but because it captures universal struggles – balancing individuality with collective harmony, adapting to unforeseen change, and the endless negotiations required to make relationships work. It offers an exaggerated yet relatable metaphor for adulthood itself:

- Learning to compromise
- Navigating evolving roles
- Finding the joy in imperfection
- Redemption following mistakes.

Much like the Brady household, modern adult life is rarely straightforward. Whether blending families, careers, or dreams, or managing the ever-shifting dynamics of relationships, adulthood is a symphony of improvisation.

In our story, Shey must confront the reality that assumptions he has made about his personal life are no longer accurate. His beloved uncle is rushed to hospital, which sparks worries about mortality. His group of friends have become dispersed. He has neglected his romantic relationship, working on assumptions that are dispelled only when his partner announces they are off to New York. And all of this is happening simultaneously. Like an explosion of personal turmoil... alongside a professional crisis. The prospect that his career is being sabotaged by his AI assistant El, someone who Shey considers simultaneously a friend, child, business partner. We hope we did a good job of depicting the messiness of mid-career life.

Our painting of where Shey's life is at 37 is intended to illustrate the centrifugal tendency of our lives. Of how we can mistake the intimacy of our childhood and adolescence as a constant, an ever present, something eternal. The reality, however, is that as we grow older, the gravity that holds our families, friends, role models together, erodes. The bonds decay. Ever so gradually. So gradually that it can be hard to recognize it until something shocking happens.

What happens to Shey is not unusual; at least the outcomes, if not quite the exact story components, are quite common.

Many professionals in their mid-career are often overwhelmed by the challenges around them. They have progressed professionally and yet happiness didn't automatically come with it or seems fleeting. There one minute and gone the next. Being married or living with a partner means constant compromise; children need attention and lots of time; humans age, parents get old, friends follow their dreams; running a business or being an executive comes with problems and breakdowns. It can be overwhelming. So, we cope by narrowing our field of vision. We worry about one thing at a time. Consequently, we can easily neglect aspects of our life. We can stop paying attention to our jobs, family, friends, even ourselves. Too often we prioritize career and family over our own mental and physical wellbeing.

There are people, albeit a very small group, who seemingly breeze through all stages of life. Perhaps you can think of some as you read this. They are together with their partners for a very long time, have interesting careers, they have dynamic, interesting, fulfilling social lives. They are happy. We both have role models in our own families that seem to live effortlessly. What is their secret?

They all appear to have one thing in common – they are perfectly comfortable with complexity and understand that life is a process. They look beyond the individual pixels of the next achievement and milestone to see a bigger picture. They understand that while knowing where we are going is critical, being skilful navigators is just as important. They make fine adjustments for the prevailing winds, they make constant course corrections, and they are forever absorbing and recalculating, like your car's GPS when it's faced with a traffic jam.

In the previous three chapters, we wrote about:

- **Drift** and the importance of avoiding professional drift and being on autopilot. The significance of adapting career to life changes, and life to career changes, and fully embracing the reality that work and career are a part of life. There are strong interdependencies.

- **Reinvention** and the importance of being ready for change, thinking in scenarios and alternative plans. Acknowledging our love affair with status quo yet always honing learning ability and reinvention skills.

- **Business reality** and the importance of direction, focus, and clarity. The importance to accept and embrace failure as the most effective way of learning. The significance of being fast and pragmatic, and the realization that nobody – nobody – is more interested in your wellbeing and future than you are. The secret sauce is constructive self-awareness. Of being conscious and awake to the risks and opportunities.

The previous chapters explored the behavioural science that underpins our subjects before providing practical conclusions. This chapter will focus more on the practical. It's an eye-level dialogue, based on our many years of observations, trials, tribulations, experiments, failures, to arrive at some small measure of earned wisdom. Our conclusions? There are five key principles that have helped people thrive in adult life:

Principle 1: Be careful what you wish for, make well thought through choices.

Principle 2: Learn to say NO – the world is complex; your life doesn't have to be.

Principle 3: Focus is the key to success, focus on and enjoy the process.

Principle 4: Live an examined life – make conscious course corrections for new data.

Principle 5: See the humorous side of everything – don't take yourself too seriously.

1. Be careful what you wish for, make well thought through choices

Desires are powerful motivators, but they often come with unintended consequences. The things you aspire to achieve or acquire may seem ideal on the surface, but have you considered the cost – financial, emotional, or relational? For example, that dream promotion might elevate your status, but it could also increase stress or take time away from loved ones. It's essential to interrogate your wishes and ask: Why do I want this? Will it truly make me happy?

Ambitions rooted in external validation can lead to dissatisfaction. Align your goals with values that genuinely resonate with you. Be aware that every 'yes' to a wish might be a 'no' to something else important. Professionals who are *thoughtful about what they wish for* don't just find success but also peace of mind.

Life is a series of decisions, and the quality of those choices determines your trajectory. Impulse-driven decisions can derail careers and relationships, while thoughtful ones build sustainable success. Take the time to evaluate your options critically. What are the short- and long-term consequences? Seek diverse perspectives when needed but own the final choice. Rushed decisions often stem from a fear of missing out or external pressures, but clarity comes with deliberate evaluation. Whether you're choosing a job, project, or partner, ask yourself: Does this align with my values and priorities? Professionals who ground their decisions in *intentionality* stay on track towards fulfilling their potential.

2. Learn to say NO – The world is complex; your life doesn't have to be

Saying 'no' is a strength, not a weakness. In today's high-demand world, it's easy to overcommit for fear of missing opportunities or disappointing others. However, saying 'yes' dilutes your focus and can lead to burnout. Learn to identify what truly matters – both professionally and personally. When faced with a request, pause and ask: Does this align with my priorities? Will it add value to my life or career? If not, politely decline. Saying 'no' creates space for 'yes' to opportunities that truly matter. Remember, boundaries are not barriers; they're safeguards for your time, energy, and mental health.

The modern world is overwhelming with endless streams of information, choices and demands. But complexity doesn't have to rule your life. Simplicity is a strategic choice. Declutter your commitments and focus on what's essential. Learn to delegate, automate, and streamline processes where possible. A clear, intentional, conscious routine brings clarity and reduces stress. Routines can be helpful when they aren't on autopilot. Don't overthink decisions that don't matter in the long run. Complexity often stems from trying to do or be everything; instead, prioritize depth over breadth. A simplified life isn't a compromise – it's a pathway to greater fulfilment and focus.

3. Focus is the key to success, focus on and enjoy the process

In a world of distractions, focus is a superpower. It's easy to spread yourself thin, chasing multiple goals or multi-tasking, but true success comes from concentrated effort. Focus doesn't mean ignoring the facts. It doesn't mean hiding from understanding the choices, decisions, and options. It means choosing one or two priorities and giving them your full attention. Define what success looks like and create a plan to achieve it. Eliminate distractions, both external (notifications, unnecessary meetings) and internal (procrastination, perfectionism). Time-blocking and setting clear boundaries are practical tools for staying on track. Professionals who master focus not only accomplish more but also achieve higher-quality results. Remember, the ability to focus is like a muscle – the more you train it, the stronger it becomes.

4. Live an examined life – make conscious course corrections for new data

The biggest trap of our middle career years is making assumptions. Assumptions that things that used to be, still are. That people we don't see very often are in an imaginary limbo. It is fascinating but true that our minds compartmentalize and trap people in historical context. Uncle Freddy is an indestructible, endless source of wisdom. Babs is a performer who will always be satisfied with operating on a small stage. Ellen will always be available to focus on our problems when we need her.

These assumptions, while natural, mislead us. If we aren't careful, they operate like faulty waypoints. We might think of our wider network of friends, family, work colleagues as a constellation. Or imaginary breadcrumbs that we have dropped throughout our lives that provide us with a sense of direction. When we are busy attending to the latest crises at work, we don't notice that one of the stars is fading. When we are consumed by our own anxieties and stress, we don't notice when one of the breadcrumbs gets blown away.

Our course through professional life is very much dependent on having accurate information. It can become very tempting to forget to update some of your base assumptions. We are all guilty of being self-centred for much of the time. Our observation is that when we are stressed, when we are chasing something we think is important, we can become very blinkered. When we talk about focus, we don't mean we should ignore what is changing around us. There is a huge difference between being vigilant and thoughtful about what you choose to do versus retreat into a cave of isolation.

In our drift chapter we talked about the **CAFFEINE** mnemonic. We introduced it in the context of professional life. A means to take an inventory of what may be changing in your career. The same prompts may be useful in this personal dimension. Creating prompts to make sure you have challenged your assumptions. We need to invest time regularly to make sure we reorientate ourselves for the subtle changes taking place in the stars around us.

5. See the humorous side of everything – don't take yourself too seriously

The last principle is the most important – all people who breeze through life happily have this skill in abundance. Humour! Life is full of challenges, but those who approach it with humour and humility often find the journey smoother and more fulfilling. Taking yourself too seriously creates unnecessary tension and isolates you from others. Humour, on the other hand, disarms conflict, builds connections, and makes even the hardest climbs feel lighter.

Adopting a playful mindset doesn't mean avoiding responsibility – it means understanding that mistakes are part of growth, and laughter is a powerful reset button. When you can smile at a missed deadline or laugh at an awkward presentation slip-up, you show resilience and perspective. This ability inspires trust and approachability, making others more likely to follow your lead.

Professionals who weave subtle and respectful humour into their lives can enjoy better mental health and stronger relationships. They're the ones who can keep their cool under pressure, charm the room during a tough negotiation, and recover quickly from setbacks. Humour is the magic sauce that turns challenges into anecdotes and keeps you grounded while reaching for the stars. Remember, life is too short not to find joy, even in the absurdities.

'If there's anything I can't stand, it's a perfect kid.' – Alice

None of us are perfect. We started this chapter with *The Brady Bunch*. The genius that leverages the true challenges of growing up to create comic gold. Indeed, one of the truths we extract from our own experience is this lesson of humour.

However, the key takeaway we wanted to communicate with this chapter is the danger of making assumptions. Acknowledging the danger of cliché overload, it's still too tempting not to mention the 'ass' of 'U' and 'ME' adage. It is very easy for us to lose track of how our personal support networks shift over time. That as life marches on, we forget to update our facts.

We limit our attention to the one or two professional priorities in front of us and then are blindsided when events escalate. Of course, many of us are very good at juggling our immediate family, partner, children with our professional priorities. However, ask yourself when you last thought deeply about what might be going on in the lives of other important people in your personal constellation. Siblings, uncles, aunts, college professors, former work colleagues... even mothers or fathers. Was it today, this week, this month... this year?

Let us finish this chapter with some Marcia Brady wisdom: 'From now on, I'm beautiful and noble. I am Juliet!'

Be careful what you wish for!

Chapter 20

I'm Sorry, Shey... I Can't Let You Do That

A twist on the immortal (irony intended) words from HAL 9000 in *Space Odyssey*.[1] We imagine El Gin saying this to Shey as he drifted toward professional obscurity.

This book is dedicated to the subject of professional reinvention. With the backdrop of a world that seems consumed by worry, anxiety, fear even, of being imminently replaced by AI, why do so many of us withdraw into our shells? What is it that possesses us to read the following: AI is automating more and more knowledge worker jobs, over the space of the next ten years, many traditional vocations from journalism to accountancy will be decimated... and conclude the best action is to keep our heads down and hope it doesn't impact us?

This feels to us like Dodo behaviour. The woolly mammoths watching the polar ice caps retreating thinking 'no matter, we'll just keep heading north'. There is a brilliant, darkly funny book by Wendy Northcutt called *The Darwin Awards: 180 Bizarre True Stories of How Dumb Humans Have Met Their Maker*.[2] Our goal with this book is to prevent number 181 if we can.

More CAFFEINE

It's quite natural for us to lose focus on our professional goals, to let things begin to drift as we mature. The initial fire and brimstone approach is slowly replaced by a quiet satisfaction. This is the phenomenon we call *professional drift*. There are at least two causes of drift. The first is how our brains reduce repetitive tasks to a background programme. The concepts of *Boreout* and *Quiet Quitting* are derived from this dynamic. But alongside these, we also experience profound changes in our outlook, our personal context. *Life-phase* research helps explains how our perspectives naturally change and how this influences our priorities.

The antidote to *professional drift*… **CAFFEINE**.

We talked about how there are essentially two sets of people in the world. The *naifs* who go through life avoiding difficult problems and embracing a blindness to growing risks of career obsolescence. These are the people who wake up one day to a nasty surprise. Then we have you, the *sophisticates*, who recognize they are prone to behavioural traps, irrational tendencies, and difficulty seeing the wood for the trees. The sophisticates put in place mechanisms, hacks, to help them motivate themselves to make proactive course corrections.

We have combined our love of coffee with what we think is a rather apt mnemonic, **CAFFEINE**. Each letter is designed to provide you with a useful tool that you can use to help you anticipate and avoid nasty shocks in your career.

How reinvention TICKs

Recognizing that your career trajectory may be under threat from AI, or some other big inflection, is of course only half the battle. Changing course can be even more difficult than recognizing the threat. Our research suggests somewhere between 10% and 30% of people successfully reinvent themselves throughout their careers. The rest, generally, face discontinuity, career breaks, followed by continuity – what we call *transition* rather than *reinvention*.

Part of the challenge is that we have only so much emotional capacity to manage change. It is simply easier to label ourselves as one thing... we picture here a Schwarzenegger type character like the *Terminator*... crashing on regardless.[3] 'I am what I am, and *I will be back. Soon!*' In a sequel, then a sequel to the sequel... and so on.

There is an alternative. We have looked closely at what distinguishes those who do succeed in genuine reinvention. We have studied what makes them **TICK**. We believe we can all emulate these traits. We suggest combining our recommendations in the professional drift chapter with those in reinvention. The two together create a synergistic power. However, if you practice one thing, we do think there is enormous power in developing a TICK and refreshing it every five years.

Entrepreneurial success and the Friedman Doctrine

'Success is not final; failure is not fatal; it is the courage to continue that counts.' There is a poetic elegance in this popular meme attributed to Winston Churchill.[4]

However, there is probably greater utility and relevance in Andrew Grove's advice: 'The sad news is, nobody owes you a career. Your career is literally your business.'[5]

Succeeding as an entrepreneur requires specific skills – timing, patience, persistence, and constant reinvention. These must be built on an idea that solves an important customer need, wrapped in an organization that works effectively to execute, and led by someone with the self-awareness and skills to know when to encourage, coach, take risks, make demands, and when to move on.

Succeeding is complex. It requires hard work, dedication, and a little luck. In this sense there are many ingredients to success. However, there is one overarching, irresistible gravitational force – *satisfying shareholders*. Over a 40-plus-year career, you are guaranteed to face situations that feel unfair. There will be occasions where you are seduced into believing you are owed some greater loyalty, some greater personal debt by a business. It is critical that you always temper your expectations with the understanding that when the chips are down, if the business faces tough choices, the board/executive/CEO should make the decision that most benefits their shareholders. If you aren't careful, you may not see this coming.

And how do we get better at adulting?

Ultimately, adulting is hard. We know this. We are con-stantly reminded when talking with people embarking on professional life. And yet… we get selective amnesia. It's a strange phenomenon. We know it's hard but at the same time, particularly as we reach our middle career years, we forget. The obvious challenges of adulting that come with transitioning from student to professional life, from dependent to independent, are not the only 'adulting' challenges we face.

In our middle career years, we can become self-absorbed. Insular. We forget that much of our lives, much of how we navigate through life, is built on a series of assumptions. Some of those we hardwire into our brains in our childhood. We lock them away in the false assumption they are eternal. Then, at some stage, we are shocked to learn they have shifted, or worse, gone away.

A key challenge for us in our middle career years is to find ways to challenge these assumptions. To ensure we have up-to-date data. To understand their implications. To adjust our personal constellations to make sure we aren't navigating by the wrong stars. After all, we shouldn't be too surprised if we get lost if we follow a faulty map.

Losing marbles

Finally, as you may remember, our goal is to entertain… and help at least one person achieve a better career outcome. The story component of *Artificial Death of a Career* is a central part of our writing purpose. Shey Sinope has become much beloved by us and others. We hope you enjoyed the latest instalment in his professional journey.

The core of this book's story is the danger of blind faith.[6] A career crisis that many of us experience in our middle and late careers. The murder mystery frame for our story seemed to choose itself. Finding your career 'murdered' is a dramatic way to amplify the point. Our use of the Elgin Marbles metaphor developed as we thought about how to sow clues about what AI was and wasn't, while also depicting some of its acknowledged risks.

We have worked closely with some AI businesses and researched what academics and insiders are really saying about its current capabilities. Is AI an existential threat? We think the question might have some similarities with nuclear power. Is it dangerous? Yes. Could it kill us all? Again, yes. However, is it an essential technology that we are going to need to leverage? Absolutely. The scaremongering about self-aware AI feels overdone... to us. However, there are undoubtedly some dangers in the unintended consequences of using AI, which is, after all, something of a black box. Using it for unpredictable, unquantifiable, nuanced problems is almost certainly at this point unwise, if not reckless.

This said, we hope that AI ends up doing for us what El Gin did for Shey. El Gin goes to enormous lengths to help Shey wake up from his sleep. Call us hopeless romantics, but perhaps AI can do the same for us in real life. Wouldn't it be wonderful to think AI could help us solve climate problems, solve world hunger, cure cancer, live better, longer lives, and help us explore our galaxy.

- The End -

Authors' Notes

The idea for *Artificial Death of a Career* emerged from three directions that collided in early 2024. The first was during our (Drs Schuster and Oxley) long debates that reached a crescendo in the summer of 2022. We have shared aspects of this story before. We both lamented the lack of entertaining, engaging, practical career advice aimed at an underserved and under-appreciated audience of NextGen leaders. Linked to this was our frustration with the transactional nature of career advice books: *7 steps to make more money, how to interview like a champ, résumé writing for a digital age* (paraphrased titles). We were deeply concerned that all of the attention seemed to be focused on landing a well-paid job and contorting yourself to whatever got you the fastest promotion and the biggest pay raise. We wanted to write the anti-materialistic career advice book. Take the counter argument that professional life was too important and had far reaching consequences for our mental, spiritual, and emotional wellbeing to be measured only by money and status.

As part of those debates, we kept distilling the long list of professional life lessons we all experience into major themes. We spent a great deal of time looking at the history of human development, our life phases, and trying to plot those into career terms. Our hypothesis was that there were four or five major transitions and challenges that we all must face. Events that were more eternal than short-term business cycles or adoption of new technology like AI. The deeper intrinsic, almost spiritual challenges, that are core to the human condition. Consequences of humans' uniquely conscious thinking capabilities.

One of these was the need to reinvent ourselves. To adapt, to evolve, to improve and develop. We knew from our own experiences in coaching others and from our research studies that significant reinventions, something more than a change of job or even geography, were increasingly important. Indeed, evidence suggested they helped us retain a certain vitality, urgency, and energy in our broader lives. We are at our best when we are chasing something elusive… *atelic*. Learning something about ourselves. Pushing our boundaries. There is lots of research evidence that underlines how succeeding in this challenge is a factor behind the so-called 'blue zones' around the world.[1] The zones where humans seem to be able to live healthier, longer.

Another strand was the idea that storytelling, works of fiction, were powerful ways to convey ideas and promote introspection. So, we wondered how we might use storytelling differently. Something like *Who Moved My Cheese* or *Little Prince* but designed for a more modern audience.[2,3] Something that would have been written had Douglas Adams, Terry Pratchett and Richard Osman met some old hippy human resources executives and social scientists for a working lunch. Something much more fun, engaging, and interesting than just setting out the science, sharing anecdotes, and offering some frameworks. So, we said, what would a book or a *series* of books look like that used a storytelling vehicle in this vein as the *central* premise? That was a big breakthrough.

What followed was our own attempts to stretch what little writing talent we have to achieve those goals. Strangely, our lack of talent didn't stop us from dreaming big. 'Well…' we said, 'If we are going to tell some stories… what format should they take?' and one of us said, '*All* of them of course!'

So, in our first book we told a ghost story, the second a time-warp repeating the same day, and the third… well… murder mystery just seemed to fit the subject matter perfectly. A story involving a career… centred on the dangers of obsolescence… and following an arc that entertainingly shared the risks of getting caught out by sleepwalking in our middle careers. We have seen, sadly, repeatedly, how after establishing ourselves and discovering who we are, of getting comfortable and more secure in our own skins, how easy it can become for people in their late 30s or early 40s to start to drift… professionally… and to lose focus.

Artificial Death of a Career emerged as a concept in early 2024. We have both worked closely with businesses using AI in innovative ways. We are both fans of sci-fi and love the related stories that are now engrained in our consciousness. Wouldn't it be fun, we thought, to try to tell a story that played on the pervasive fears about AI, while dispelling the scaremongering exaggerations, and at the same time use it as a metaphor for how our personal reinventions are deeper and more complex than simply learning to use new tools.

What is interesting to us is that Shey Sinope resonates with so many people. We are occasionally asked if he represents one or both of us. Of course you write from experience, but Shey is a photofit, a legion, of all the people we have ever worked with and ourselves. And what happens in this book is as much a reflection of the strange alchemy that seems to mysteriously emerge from the page, once you unleash your imagination.

We both had an ambition to see Shey through five or six books. Five or six adventures. If books one and two had not found an audience, then we may have stopped. Spared the world from our rambling, irreverent, eccentric humour and attempts at wisdom. However, if you're reading this, then we suppose our books have found an audience and you are at least partially to blame for encouraging us. We won't spoil the surprise for the format and premise for book four… suffice to say we will continue to reach to meld fiction genres with our rather niche attempts at providing NextGen professionals with a fresh reading alternative.

Incidentally, let us end these notes with a proposal. In our more expansive moments, we like to imagine that perhaps our approach is a new category. Neither non-fiction nor fiction. Not narrative non-fiction, or pure business leadership, or professional life advice. We are proud of not fitting in a box. After all, being pan-genre is liberating. However, if friends of yours ask what sort of book you're reading we suggest you say it's a *Professional Advice Narrative Tales*. We like the idea of them eventually realizing that the acronym is PANTs. What better way to end these notes than on that one!

Acknowledgements

This book wouldn't be possible without all of the people we have both worked with over the years. The people at BP, Reliance Industries, E&Y, Ivoclar, AFS, and the extraordinary entrepreneurial talent we have had the privilege to advise. We have learned so much in working with people in the USA, UK, India, UAE, Austria, Lichtenstein, and countless other places. We have attempted to distil and do justice to the enormous wisdom you have shared with us over the past 40 years.

We couldn't have written this book without the training, support, and inspiration from some noteworthy teachers. Dr Oxley would like to thank Jim McNeish, Dr Lockey, Dr Buchanan, Dr Pilbeam, and Dr Vyakarnam. David would like to acknowledge the radical thinking of Shri Mukesh Ambani and Dr Gary Hamel. Dr Schuster would like to acknowledge two of his teachers: Professor Först, he made me appreciate and better understand some of the world's great writers, and Professor Alexander van der Bellen, who taught me the importance and value of independent thinking while completing my PhD in Vienna.

Over the last five years we have both immersed ourselves in the world of machine learning, what is often referred to as AI. It presents incredible potential to solve some complex and important problems. This book and its central storyline owes a debt to the knowledge and experience we have gained with start-up entrepreneurs in the AI space, in particular Anand Verma and Felix

Henderson. During this same period, we have also enjoyed and learned a great deal from the work and writings of Michael Wooldridge and Janelle Shane.[1,2] If you are looking to deepen your AI knowledge, we recommend choosing one of their books next.

A very special thanks is reserved for Dr Angelos Gkanoutas-Leventis for his friendship, and education on all things Greek. Thank you also to Violetta who proved the limitations of the *girlfriend operating system* and so skilfully moulded our friend into the all-conquering renewable energy executive (and possibly detective) he has become.

Both Drs Schuster and Oxley would like to thank Practical Inspiration Publishing. Specific thanks to Alison Jones, Shell Cooper, and Lizzie Evans. It's been an absolute pleasure and education to work with such professional, talented people.

Special thanks once again go to Andy (Doodles) Baker for his amazing illustrations and to Rachel Moulton for her early encouragement when Shey was still stuck in his dorm room.

A *special dedication* from Dr Schuster to the people who helped him create and encouraged him to build Chirimoya.com. It has transcended all expectations to emerge as something vibrant and extraordinary. Thanks to Didier, who always encouraged me to pursue my dreams, Jonathan, Mari, Ruben, Freddie, Yvonne, and Zakaria. A very big thank you to Sir Ian Davis, who continued to be such a great inspiration and thought partner long after our time with bp.

A *special dedication* from Dr Oxley to Sue. For each of our books I have made a point of thanking Sue for her unwavering love and support. And for my daughters for all their encouragement and occasional testing of concepts. I've made a point also of thanking Fynn and Lane for their reminder that imagination, creativity, and fun are always there… even though we sometimes forget where we put them when we get older. I do so again here because the thanks are no less heartfelt, and their support is no less vital. I love you all.

Finally, posthumously to my parents Terry and Shirley. Yes, *it is writing… just not as we know it.*

Supplementary Notes

Introduction

[1] A. Graham (2023). *One in three workers fear AI could take their jobs.* Independent. www.independent.co.uk/business/one-in-three-workers-fear-ai-could-take-their-jobs-b2438335.html

[2] C. Vallance (2023). *AI could replace equivalent of 300 million jobs – report.* BBC. www.bbc.co.uk/news/technology-65102150

[3] Hazan et al. (2024). *A new future of work: The race to deploy AI.* McKinsey Global Institute. www.mckinsey.com/mgi/our-research/a-new-future-of-work-the-race-to-deploy-ai-and-raise-skills-in-europe-and-beyond#

[4] R. Florisson (2024). *The UK insecure work index 2024.* Lancaster University. Work Foundation. www.lancaster.ac.uk/media/lancaster-university/content-assets/images/lums/work-foundation/UKInsecureWorkIndex2024.pdf

[5] J.M. Alkhalifah et al. (2024). 'Existential anxiety about AI' in *Front Psychiatry.* www.ncbi.nlm.nih.gov/pmc/articles/PMC11036542/

[6] C. Clifford (2018). *Google CEI: AI is more important that fire or electricity.* CNBC. www.cnbc.com/2018/02/01/google-ceo-sundar-pichai-ai-is-more-important-than-fire-electricity.html#

[7] A.C. Clarke (1968). *2001: A Space Odyssey.* New American Library.

[8] N. Massey (2013). *Humans may be the most adaptive species.* Scientific American. Environment & Energy Publishing. www.scientificamerican.com/article/humans-may-be-most-adaptive-species/

[9] L.C. Megginson (1963). 'Lessons from Europe for American business' in *Southwestern Social Science Quarterly.*

[10] W.B. Cannon (1929). *Bodily Changes in Pain, Hunger, Fear and Rage.* Appleton

[11] D. Mobbs et al. (2015). 'The ecology of human fear: Survival optimization and the nervous system' in *Frontiers in Neuroscience.* www.ncbi.nlm.nih.gov/pmc/articles/PMC4364301/

[12] PwC (2013). *17th Annual Global CEO Survey: The talent challenge.* https://preview.thenewsmarket.com/Previews/PWC/DocumentAssets/330782.pdf

[13] Fountech.ai (2019). *30 million Brits want to learn a new skill, yet half will never act on their intentions.* www.fenews.co.uk/skills/30-million-brits-want-to-learn-a-new-skill-yet-over-half-will-never-act-on-their-intentions

[14] S. London (2019). *How to double the odds that your change program will succeed.* McKinsey. www.mckinsey.com/capabilities/people-and-organizational-performance/our-insights/how-to-double-the-odds-that-your-change-program-will-succeed#/

[15] T. Kulash (2013). *Many stroke, heart-attack survivors make no changes after event.* Medical Xpress. https://medicalxpress.com/news/2013-08-heart-attack-survivors-event.html

[16] Drs Schuster & Oxley (2025). See all our latest career articles at: www.drsschusterandoxley.com/news

Chapter 2

[1] S. Rose (2023). *Five ways AI might destroy the world: 'Everyone on Earth could fall over dead in the same second'.* The Guardian. www.theguardian.com/technology/2023/jul/07/five-ways-ai-might-destroy-the-world-everyone-on-earth-could-fall-over-dead-in-the-same-second

[2] J. Chen (2024). *Unicorn: What it means in investing.* Investopedia. www.investopedia.com/terms/u/unicorn.asp

[3] S. Fry and C. Hitchens (2009). *The Catholic Church is a force for good in the world.* www.intelligencesquared.com/events/the-catholic-church-is-a-force-for-good-in-the-world/

[4] T. Jones and T. Gilliam (1975). *Monty Python and the Holy Grail.* www.youtube.com/watch?v=yp_l5ntikaU

[5] D. Adams (1980). *The Hitchhikers Guide to the Galaxy.* Harmony Books.

Chapter 4

[1] Seasonal Affective Disorder. Overview of SAD. NHS. www.nhs.uk/mental-health/conditions/seasonal-affective-disorder-sad/overview/

Chapter 8

[1] OAIC – Office of the Australian Information Commissioner.

[2] Troy Hunt (2013). *Have I Been Pwned* is a phishing and privacy tracking site. https://haveibeenpwned.com

Chapter 11

[1] J.H. Tiltman (2002). *The most mysterious manuscript in the world.* www.nsa.gov/portals/75/documents/news-features/declassified-documents/tech-journals/voynich-manuscript-mysterious.pdf

Chapter 13

[1] H.W.J. Rittel and M.M. Webber (1973). 'Dilemmas in general theory of planning' in *Policy Sciences.* https://link.springer.com/article/10.1007/bf01405730

[2] T. G. Plante (2014). 'Giving people advice rarely works, this does' in *Psychology Today.* There is no consensus on the actual percentage of 'good advice' that is rejected. However, we generally accept that humans' behaviours and

routines are better changed by less direct approaches. www.psychologytoday.com/intl/blog/do-the-right-thing/201407/giving-people-advice-rarely-works-does

Chapter 14

[1] Remember the FAST acronym to recognize early signs of a stroke. Be an advocate and learn more at: www.england.nhs.uk/2023/03/stroke-survivors-and-their-savers-call-on-people-to-act-f-a-s-t-as-part-of-nhs-campaign/#:~:text=The%20F.A.S.T.,(T)%20to%20call%20999

[2] Transient ischemic attack (TIA). NHS. www.nhs.uk/conditions/transient-ischaemic-attack-tia/causes/#:~:text=In%20TIAs%2C%20the%20blockage%20quickly,brain%20and%20longer%2Dterm%20problems

[3] Hypertension Treatments. NHS. www.nhs.uk/conditions/high-blood-pressure/

[4] Inc. (2016). *50 inspirational pieces of wisdom from Muhammad Ali*. www.inc.com/gordon-tredgold/muhammad-ali-50-inspiring-thoughts-from-the-greatest-of-all-time.html

[5] M. Muchmore (2024). macOS vs. Windows: Which OS really is the best? *PCMAG*. www.pcmag.com/news/macos-vs-windows-which-os-really-is-the-best

Chapter 15

[1] J. Collins (2001). *Good to Great: Why Some Companies Make the Leap and Others Don't*. Harper Business.

[2] A. Grove (1996). *Only the Paranoid Survive*. Doubleday Press.

[3] J. Kotter (2016). *Leading Change*. Harvard Business School Press.

[4] S. Ismail, M.S. Malone and Y. van Geest (2014). *Exponential Organizations*. Diversion Books.

[5] C. Christensen (2016). *The Innovator's Dilemma. Management of Innovation and Change*. Harvard Business Review Press.

[6] M.E. Porter (1985). *The Competitive Advantage*. Free Press.

[7] W. Isaacson (2011). *Steve Jobs*. Abacus.

[8] P. Knight (2016). *Shoe Dog*. Simon & Schuster.

[9] R. Kroc and R. Anderson (2016). *Grinding It Out: The Making of McDonald's*. St Martin's Publishing.

[10] M. Lewis (2011). *The Big Short*. W.W. Norton. M. Lewis (1989). *Liar's Poker*. W. W. Norton.

[11] J.J. Arnett (2016). 'Life stage concepts across history and cultures: Proposal for a new field on indigenous life stages' in *Human Development*. https://karger.com/hde/article-abstract/59/5/290/158055/Life-Stage-Concepts-across-History-and-Cultures?redirectedFrom=fulltext

[12] G. Sheehy (1974). *Passages: Predicable Crises of Adult Life*. Dutton.

[13] E.H. Erikson (1959). *Identity and Life Cycle*. International Universities Press.

[14] R.L. Gould (1978). *Transformations: Growth and Change in Adult Life*. Simon & Schuster.

[15] J. Ewing (2019). *Where there's always a giraffe*. Business 101. https://business101.com/an-ai-expert-explains-why-theres-always-a-giraffe-in-artificial-intelligence/

[16] M. Wooldridge (2021). *A Brief History of Artificial Intelligence*. Flatiron Books.

Chapter 16

[1] D. Oxley and H. Schuster (2024). *Finding your first job after school*. SecEd. www.sec-ed.co.uk/content/best-practice/finding-your-first-job-after-school-three-exercises/

[2] P. Rothlin and P.R. Werder (2008). *Boreout! Overcoming Workplace Demotivation*. Kogan Page.

[3] J. Harter (2022). *Is quiet quitting real? Gallup*. www.gallup.com/workplace/398306/quiet-quitting-real.aspx

[4] B. Andreatta (2017). *Wired to Resist: The Brain Science of Why Change Fails and a New Model for Driving Success*. 7th Mind Publishing.

[5] O. Hikosaka (2024). 'Dopamine Neurons Encoding Long-Term Memory of Object Value for Habitual Behavior' in *NIH*. https://pubmed.ncbi.nlm.nih.gov/26590420/

[6] G. Sheehy (1974). *Passages: Predictable Crises of Adult Life*. Dutton.

[7] D.G. Blanchflower and A.J. Oswald (2000). 'Well-being over time in Britain and the USA' in *NBER*. www.nber.org/papers/w7487

[8] D.E. Super (1957). *The Psychology of Careers*. Harper.

[9] Drs Schuster and Oxley (2025). *A Groundhog Career*. Practical Inspiration Publishing.

[10] K. Setiya (2018). *Midlife: A Philosophical Guide*. Princeton University Press.

[11] K. Chayka (2023). *Rethinking the luddites in the age of AI*. The New Yorker. www.newyorker.com/books/page-turner/rethinking-the-luddites-in-the-age-of-ai

[12] StickK commit. A digital tool designed to help you achieve goals. www.stickk.com/tour

[13] Beeminder. Another digital tool designed to help you achieve personal goals. www.beeminder.com

[14] D.A. Cobb-Clark et al. (2024). 'Sophistication about self-control' in *Journal of Public Economics*. www.sciencedirect.com/science/article/pii/S0047272724001324#:~:text=Specifically%2C%20there%20is%20a%20correspondence,then%20fail%20to%20do%20so

[15] P. La Duke (2024). Drs Schuster and Oxley on the top five trends to watch in the future of work. *Authority Magazine*. https://medium.com/authority-magazine/drs-schuster-and-oxley-on-the-top-five-trends-to-watch-in-the-future-of-work-9a12e7d835cd

Chapter 17

[1] L. Bodel (2022). *Most change initiatives fail – Here's how to beat the odds.* Forbes. www.forbes.com/sites/lisabodell/2022/03/28/most-change-initiatives-fail---heres-how-to-beat-the-odds/?

[2] M. Vanhoenacker (2023). *A journey across London on the Elizabeth line.* New York Times. www.nytimes.com/2023/05/30/travel/elizabeth-line-london.html?smid=url-share

[3] L. Pauwels, S. Chalavi and S. P. Swinnen (2018). 'Aging and brain plasticity' in *National Library of Medicine.* https://pmc.ncbi.nlm.nih.gov/articles/PMC6128435/

[4] T. Chamorro-Premuzic (2014). 'Why are older people more conservative?' in *Psychology Today.* www.psychologytoday.com/us/blog/mr-personality/201410/why-are-older-people-more-conservative

[5] J. Panksepp (1998). *Affective Neuroscience: The Foundations of Human and Animal Emotions.* Oxford University Press.

[6] S. Freud (1920). 'Development of the libido and sexual organizations' in S. Freud, *A General Introduction to Psychoanalysis.* Horace Liveright.

[7] J. Bowlby (1973). *Attachment and Loss.* Basic Books.

[8] C. Hazan and P.R. Shaver (1990). 'Love and work: An attachment-theoretical perspective' in *Journal of Personality and Social Psychology.* https://psycnet.apa.org/buy/1991-00927-001

[9] I. Ivanova (2023). *Most laid-off workers today quickly find new jobs.* CBS News. www.cbsnews.com/news/layoff-workers-how-are-they-doing/

[10] J. Pollak (2023). *Survey of recently laid-off workers.* ZipRecruiter. www.ziprecruiter.com/blog/survey-of-recently-laid-off-workers/

[11] A. Kade (2020). *Should you ever take a pay cut?* The Muse. www.themuse.com/advice/should-you-ever-take-a-pay-cut

[12] M.I. Finney (2009). *Rebound: A Proven Plan for Starting Over After Job Loss.* FT Press.

[13] R. Bolles (2022). *What Color is Your Parachute?* Ten Speed Press.

[14] W. Bridges (2019). *Transitions: Making Sense of Life's Changes.* Da Capo Press.

[15] P. La Duke (2024). *Drs Schuster and Oxley on the top five trends to watch in the future of work.* Authority Magazine. https://medium.com/authority-magazine/drs-schuster-and-oxley-on-the-top-five-trends-to-watch-in-the-future-of-work-9a12e7d835cd

[16] J. Gribbin (2004). *The Scientists: A History of Science Told Through the Lives of Its Greatest Inventors.* Random House.

[17] D. Gross (1996). *Forbes Greatest Business Stories of All Time.* John Wiley & Sons.

[18] P. Pompliano (2023). *Hidden Genius: The Secret Ways of Thinking That Power the World's Most Successful People.* Harriman House.

[19] M. Conefrey (2006). *The Adventurer's Handbook: Life Lessons from History's Great Explorers.* Collins.

[20] Drs Schuster and Oxley (2025). *A Groundhog Career*. Practical Inspiration Publishing.

[21] K. Setiya (2018). *Midlife: A Philosophical Guide*. Princeton University Press.

[22] Drs Schuster and Oxley (2025). *A Groundhog Career*. Practical Inspiration Publishing.

[23] K. Milkman (2021). *How to Change: The Science of Getting from Where You Are to Where You Want to Be*. Portfolio.

[24] C. Heath and D. Heath (2010). *Switch: How to Change Things When Change Is Hard*. Broadway Books.

[25] K. Lewin (1948). *Resolving Social Conflicts and Field Theory in Social Science*. Harper & Row.

[26] C. Gallo (2019). *The tote bag that goes everywhere with Bill Gates*. Forbes. www.forbes.com/sites/carminegallo/2019/09/27/the-tote-bag-that-goes-everywhere-with-bill-gates-holds-the-secret-to-his-success/

[27] M. Urwin (2024). *AI taking over jobs: What to know about the future of jobs*. Builtin.com. https://builtin.com/artificial-intelligence/ai-replacing-jobs-creating-jobs

[28] D.F. Runde, L. Sandin and A. Kohan (2021). *Addressing an aging population through digital transformation in the Western Hemisphere*. CSIS. www.csis.org/analysis/addressing-aging-population-through-digital-transformation-western-hemisphere#:~:text=Aging%20in%20the%20Western%20Hemisphere,the%20end%20of%20the%20century

[29] G. Michael and S. Armstrong (2015). *How Innovation and Technology Has Lowered The Barrier to Entry Like Never Before*. Forbes. www.forbes.com/sites/jpmorganchase/2015/11/03/how-innovation-and-technology-has-lowered-the-barrier-to-entry-like-never-before/#:~:text=The%20advent%20of%20cloud%20technologies,and%20ecosystem%20around%20their%20business

Chapter 18

[1] P. Voice (2011). *Rawls Explained: From Fairness to Utopia (Ideas Explained)*. Open Court.

[2] J. Stillman (2016). *Just 3 percent of universities produce 90 percent of Unicorns*. Inc. www.inc.com/jessica-stillman/unicorn-breeders-these-universities-produce-90-percent-of-super-successful-found.html

[3] F.W. Taylor (1911). *The Principles of Scientific Management*. Harper and Brothers.

[4] C.I. Barnard (1938). *The Functions of the Executive*. Harvard University Press.

[5] T. Levitt (1960). 'Marketing Myopia' in *Harvard Business Review*. https://nadiamarketing.com.br/site/wp-content/uploads/2019/01/mrketingmiopia41336.pdf

[6] J. Collins (2001). *Good to Great: Why Some Companies Make the Leap... and Others Don't*. Harper Business.

[7] E. Ries (2011). *The Lean Startup: How Today's Entrepreneurs Use Continuous Innovation to Create Radically Successful Business*. Crown Business.

8 S. Landsburg (2019). *The Essential Milton Friedman (Essential Scholars)*. Fraser Institute.

9 P. Calma (2024). 'The Rapid Rise of Revolut' in *Trinity Business Review*. https://tbr.ie/2024/10/02/the-rapid-rise-of-revolut/#:~:text=The%20story%20 behind%20Revolut%20is,world's%20most%20valuable%20fintech%20companies

10 J. Cook (2020). *How Gymshark became a $1.3 Billion Brand*. Forbes. www.forbes.com/sites/jodiecook/2020/08/17/how-gymshark-became-a-13bn-brand-and-what-we-can-learn/

11 P. Westberg (2024). 'The rise of Meta' in *Quartr*. https://quartr.com/insights/company-research/the-rise-of-meta-from-dorm-room-to-global-dominance

12 US Bureau of Labor Statistics. www.bls.gov/opub/ted/2024/34-7-percent-of-business-establishments-born-in-2013-were-still-operating-in-2023.htm

13 Bain & Company (2023). *Under 1% of unicorns are profiting at scale*. www.bain.com/about/media-center/press-releases/2023/under-1-of-unicorns-are-profiting-at-scale-with-true-business-success-despite-$1-billion-plus-valuationsbain--company-analysis/

14 M. Juetten (2019). *Failed startups: Jawbone*. Forbes. www.forbes.com/sites/maryjuetten/2019/02/05/failed-startups-jawbone/

15 A. Shontell (2013). 'After raising $1.8 million Tutorspree shuts down' in *Business Insider*. www.businessinsider.com/tutorspree-shuts-down-2013-9

16 S.A. O'Brien (2022). *The rise and fall of Theranos*. CNN. www.cnn.com/2022/07/07/tech/theranos-rise-and-fall/index.html

17 E. Rella (2024). *Woman goes viral after recording her disastrous call with HR after being let go*. Entrepreneur. www.entrepreneur.com/business-news/woman-goes-viral-for-live-recording-her-layoff-talking-back/468422

18 J. Kelly (2022). *CEO who fired 900 employees via a zoom call*. Forbes. www.forbes.com/sites/jackkelly/2022/03/09/ceo-who-fired-900-employees-via-a-zoom-video-and-called-his-employees-dumb-dolphins-had-a-mass-layoff-some-workers-found-out-by-seeing-their-bank-account/

19 D.M. Phelps (2006). *Businesspeople are evil!* Acton Institute. https://rlo.acton.org/archives/1034-businesspeople-are-evil.html

20 J. Tucker (2010). *Jill Brown on why corporations get branded as evil*. PhysOrg. https://phys.org/news/2010-12-jill-brown-corporations-branded-evil.html

21 P. Toynbee (2003). *Fat cats pay is the result of greed*. Guardian. www.theguardian.com/politics/2003/dec/24/economy.executivesalaries

Chapter 19

1 S. Schwartz (1971). *The Brady Bunch*. ABC.

2 M. Twain (2012). *Mark Twain at Your Fingertips: A Book of Quotations*, p. 190, Courier Corporation.

Chapter 20

[1] A.C. Clarke (1968). *2001: A Space Odyssey*. New American Library.

[2] W. Northcutt (2001). *The Darwin Awards: 180 Bizarre True Stories of How Dumb Humans Have Met Their Maker*. Orion Paperbacks.

[3] M. Lee (2016). *The definitive Terminator*. Overthinking It. www.overthinkingit.com/2016/05/24/definitive-terminator-analysis/

[4] International Churchill Society (2024). Quotes falsely attributed to Winston Churchill. https://winstonchurchill.org/resources/quotes/quotes-falsely-attributed/

[5] A. Grove (1999). *Only the Paranoid Survive*. Currency Doubleday.

[6] Drs Schuster and Oxley (2023). *A Career Carol*. Austin Macauley.

Authors' Notes

[1] Blue Zones. *Living longer, better*. Access more information at: www.bluezones.com

[2] S. Johnson (1999). *Who Moved My Cheese*. Vermilion.

[3] A. De Saint Exupery (1943). *The Little Prince*. Reynal & Hitchcock.

Acknowledgements

[1] M. Wooldridge (2021). *A Brief History of Artificial Intelligence*. Flatiron Books.

[2] J. Shane (2019). *You Look Like a Thing, and I Love You*. Voracious.

Index

A quick word from Practical Inspiration Publishing...

We hope you found this book both practical and inspiring – that's what we aim for with every book we publish.

We publish titles on topics ranging from leadership, entrepreneurship, HR and marketing to self-development and wellbeing.

Find details of all our books at: www.practicalinspiration.com

 Did you know...

We can offer discounts on bulk sales of all our titles – ideal if you want to use them for training purposes, corporate giveaways or simply because you feel these ideas deserve to be shared with your network.

We can even produce bespoke versions of our books, for example with your organization's logo and/or a tailored foreword.

To discuss further, contact us on info@practicalinspiration.com.

 **Got an idea for a business book?**

We may be able to help. Find out about more about publishing in partnership with us at: bit.ly/PIpublishing.

Follow us on social media...

 @PIPTalking

@pip_talking

@practicalinspiration

@piptalking

Practical Inspiration Publishing